# LIFE AND TRADITION IN
# RURAL IRELAND

# LIFE & TRADITION
## in
# RURAL IRELAND

## by Timothy P. O'Neill

with a map
22 drawings in text
and 142 photographs

LONDON: J. M. DENT & SONS LTD

First published 1977

Printed in Great Britain by
Butler & Tanner Ltd
Frome and London
for J. M. DENT & SONS LTD
Aldine House, Albemarle Street, London

This book is set in 12 on 14 point Garamond

British Library Cataloguing in Publication Data
O'Neill, Timothy
    Life and tradition in rural Ireland.
    1. Ireland—Social life and customs
    I. Title
    941.7082'4        DA959.1

ISBN 0 460 04227 0

# Contents

# Photographs

# Drawings

*Abbreviations*

N.M.I.  National Museum of Ireland.
N.L.I.  National Library of Ireland.
I.F.C.  Irish Folklore Commission, Department of Irish Folklore, University College, Dublin.
B.F.  Bord Failte Eireann (Irish Tourist Board).

# IRELAND

Scale: 27 Miles to One Inch

10 5 0    10    20    30    40    50    60    70    80    90    100 Miles

© Government of Ireland 1965.

O.S.O. Dublin 1965.

# Introduction

The pace of modern life has made much of the subject matter of this book anachronistic. Life in Ireland has been urbanized and mechanized and the old folk ways are now a thing of the past. The material culture of the old days has vanished and that which survives is often treasured for its curiosity value rather than its use. The lives of the ordinary people of rural Ireland are now similar to those of their peers in most western European countries and only the landscape, monuments and chance survivals of artefacts show how different life was only a short time ago. This book examines some basic elements of life and tradition in rural Ireland through the ages.

The recording of everyday objects of daily life was begun early enough for two fine collections to be made in museums in Dublin and Belfast and these will prove a golden treasure for future generations in Ireland. These objects will show the pattern of development of daily life and it will be seen that man's struggle for survival was hard, that living conditions were uncomfortable and that material comforts were few. The rate of change in rural Ireland was slow, but since 1945 there has been a revolution in all aspects of life on the land. Changing population patterns, improved housing, heating, lighting and roads and, more recently, greater prosperity and extended educational opportunities have all led to the abandoning of the old ways. Modern machinery has made the homely tools, implements and objects of antiquity obsolete in the last thirty years. It is the artefacts and way of life of the pre-1945 era which are examined here.

Many objects of everyday use are not described and this has always been the case. Objects excavated from archaeological sites can sometimes only be explained by reference to modern usage, and so many of the simple artefacts of the pre-1945 era are important. Despite Ireland's rich oral tradition there is a paucity of material remains of everyday life for many centuries. There is hardly a complete house in Ireland which can be traced back with certainty to medieval times. Yet there is a strong line of tradition between ancient and modern Ireland. This is seen clearly in the oral tradition of the people, in their beliefs, their stories, their games and also in the methods and techniques associated with their primitive crafts, agriculture and fishing. Ireland's oral tradition is well publicized, but the material culture of the country has been largely ignored except by a few writers. In this book the emphasis is placed on material culture.

Each section in this book is merely an introduction to the subject examined and each topic is worthy of far more detailed and careful research. The chapters that present material in detail can be regarded as a tribute to the handful of scholars who have laboured in the field while the other sections could possibly provide a starting point for those who wish to delve further into this fascinating subject. Three people deserve special mention—Professor E. E. Evans, Dr K. Danaher and Dr A. T. Lucas. From reading the works of these authors whose expertise I admire and whose depth of scholarship I envy, I have been able to put some structure on the experiences of my youth and on my observations as an ethnologist in the National Museum of Ireland. I owe a special debt to Dr Lucas who, as director of the Museum, encouraged me to work in this area. To him and to all my former colleagues in the Museum I owe a debt of gratitude. During my years there an interest in the past was transformed into a serious quest for knowledge about all aspects of life and tradition in Ireland in all ages. Of all my former colleagues my greatest debt is to Catherine Treacy who drew most of the illustrations in this book and without which it would be much poorer. To her, Brendan Storey and Dermot O'Sullivan, all of whom worked with me on the folk life collections, I offer my thanks.

In writing a work of this kind many debts are incurred. I wish to record my gratitude to M. F. Ryan and P. Wallace for answering numerous queries. I wish to thank P. Wallace for his constructive comments on the typescript before publication. My thanks to J. G. Delaney and M. J. Murphy for their help on many enjoyable field trips and for introducing me to so many great country characters. I would like to thank B. Doyle, M. Cleary and May Boyd for their help with photographs and also the many librarians who were always patient, helpful and courteous. I wish to thank Bord Fáilte Éireann and the National Museum of Ireland for permission to use photographs from their collections. I thank Bríd Duignan for her typing. G. Jenkins of the Welsh Folk Museum I thank for suggesting I write this book and for giving me the opportunity to do so, and finally I am grateful, as always, for the encouragement and help of my wife.

I belong to a generation reared when rural traditions were strong. Though steeped in this tradition we have done little to carry it on and indeed we have seen the old ways altered and the old beliefs forgotten. In the modern world it is impossible for rural dwellers to be as isolated as their ancestors. The counter-attractions have beaten storytelling and other traditional amusements into inferior positions. Yet no one who has experienced the bitter sweet pleasures of stories about ghosts, fairies or daemon cocks guarding mythical treasures beneath mysterious mounds could ever get the same pleasure from commercially produced shows. The line of tradition has been broken, yet there are signs that many young people are today beginning to realize both the enjoyment and cultural value of such ways and a revival of interest in these aspects may yet be seen. It is hoped that this book may give glimpses of that past.

To my father, who unhappily died before this work was finished, and to my mother I dedicate this book. It was they who first introduced me to the many ways and the wiles of rural Ireland.

T. P. O'N.
Lonagh Cottage,
Co. Cork

Lughnasa, 1976

# 1 Houses

No aspect of material folk culture in Ireland has attracted more attention from the layman or the scholar than the traditional house. The thatched house is such a familiar sight that it has become almost a symbol of national identity. Houses of this type are favourite photographic subjects for tourists, artists never seem to tire of painting them and many Irish writers have seen these humble dwellings as the ideal settings for their literary efforts. For Irish emigrants abroad and indeed for many migrants from rural to urban Ireland they symbolize the past and a way of life which is rapidly disappearing.

What is this house which has attracted so much attention? To the casual observer all Irish traditional houses appear as long low buildings with thatched roofs and whitewashed walls. Most of the houses are built of stone, clay or mud and to a lesser extent sod or turf,[1] and the rooms are invariably arranged in length with a door from one leading to the next. The roof is generally at an angle of 45 degrees to the walls and the roof timbers usually sit on the walls, though cruck roofs and purlin roofs are also known. Windows and doors are usually found in side walls rather than in the ends, and the hearth, which lies on the long axis of the house, is normally at floor level. The chimney projects through the roof ridge[2] (fig. 1). Traditional slate and stone roofed houses also have the same characteristics though slate roofs were found in few districts. Shingles or overlapping wooden tiles are recorded also in some northern counties.[3]

In terms of traditional houses which are still occupied the earliest extant examples probably date from the seventeenth century. For knowledge of earlier house types archaeological excavation must be relied upon. Ground plans, building materials and the position of the hearth are all that can be given with certainty, but there are exceptions to this. Corbelled structures in the west and south-west are known to exist for a long period in a complete state as are the medieval tower houses of the Anglo-Norman chiefs. Habitation sites in some areas show evidence of continuous occupation from earliest times to the present day. In the Lough Gur district of Co. Limerick a series of houses from Neolithic to modern times has been

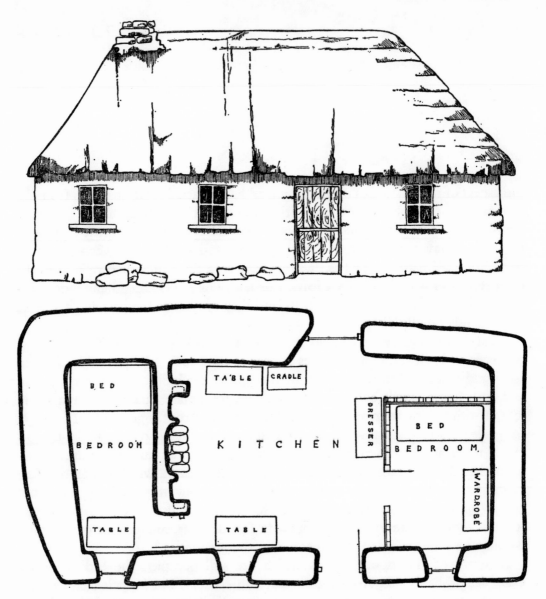

*Fig. 1. Traditional house, Menlough, Co. Galway.*

excavated and recorded.[4] Other types of site also show signs of long periods of occupation. *Crannógs* or artificial islands on lakes were inhabited at various periods from the Bronze Age to the seventeenth century, while *raths* or ring forts, which were introduced during the Iron Age, were also inhabited till the seventeenth century.[5] Ireland's first settlers, the Mesolithic hunters and fishermen, have left little evidence of their habitation sites except for hearths. The earliest house sites, extensively excavated, date from the Neolithic and Bronze Ages. The dozen or so houses at Lough Gur, Co. Limerick, were both round and rectangular in plan and each had a stone base with light timber uprights supporting wattle or sod walls. From post holes discovered during excavation it is assumed that the roof was supported on wooden posts. These posts divided the interior of the houses along the length of the two lines of posts, each about 4 feet from the central axis, and formed what is known as an aisled house.[6] Ancient refuse dumps called 'kitchen middens' also date from Neolithic times, but such sites contain few structural remains which show evidence of the type of house or hut used.

While there is evidence that single farmhouses were known in Ireland before the arrival of the Celtic speaking immigrants in the last quarter of the first millenium BC, it was only as a result of the new economy which they introduced that the single farmhouse became widespread. Following the arrival of the Celts there was a dramatic alteration in the landscape. The earliest single houses of the Iron Age were probably unenclosed, but the surviving house sites are found in defensive raths, *cashels* and hill forts. The impact of these on the rural landscape can be gauged from the fact that between thirty and forty thousand raths or ring forts of earth or stone still survive.[7] The commonest type of rath is a circular enclosure of between 60 and 100 feet in diameter surrounded by an earthen bank and fosse. In areas where stone was plentiful a dry stone wall was substituted for the earth and such structures are called cashels. The houses stood inside these defensive structures, and Proudfoot, who has studied the economy of the Irish rath, has shown that the buildings varied enormously in design and materials.[8] The houses were either circular or rectangular with rounded ends. The largest of the rectangular houses measured up to 20 feet in width and were constructed of post wattle with sod or clay walls and roofed with thatch or shingles. In contrast, in cashels, the houses were usually stone built. Houses in a rath represented on an early seventeenth-century map show sub-rectangular or oval thatched houses of both one and two storeys. In some of these map representations chimneys are clearly shown while other houses appear to have no chimneys.[9] Some had solid walls, some had wattle walls and these may well be similar to the houses of the earlier period, but until further excavation has been carried out, little can be said about the evolution of house types in raths in the long period between 500 BC and AD 1700. Raths are occupied throughout this period yet the peak period of occupation appear to have been the first millennium AD.

If knowledge of raths is limited, the knowledge of hill forts and the houses in them is even more limited. It is only in recent years that extensive excavation has begun on this type of site and to date only a few houses have been discovered. At Downpatrick an oval hut was discovered and the indications are that the earliest settlements in hill forts date from the late Bronze Age.[10] Some crannógs or habitation sites on man-made islands in lakes also belong to this period. Wood-Martin listed about two hundred crannógs in Ireland in 1886 but, as sites are discovered continuously through lake levels falling because of drainage, the number now known is considerably higher.[11] Most crannógs date from the early Christian period and such sites are also defensive in nature. At Ballinderry crannóg a horseshoe-shaped house 52 feet across the widest point was discovered and was dated to the tenth century.[12] Promontory forts were current in the Iron Age and these also contain house sites. Little evidence of undefended house sites or of clustered houses has been found, though many believe that these existed in this period.[13]

The advent of Christianity brought a new type of architecture with church building. Initially, however, churches and monks' huts followed well-known patterns. Many were built of timber and sod and some clusters of monks' huts of corbelled stone are among the few examples of undefended houses.[14] The Norsemen's contribution to Ireland was to establish the first towns and their impact on rural Ireland is still an open question. They established many contacts with the earlier settlers in rural Ireland and their post and wattled aisled houses in Dublin are similar in many respects to houses of the same period in rural Ireland. The frequency of raids and conflict in Ireland in the time of the Norsemen led to further defensive building, of which the most notable examples are the round towers associated with Christian monasteries which can still be seen. These were necessary not only as defences against Norse raids as was traditionally believed, but also to protect the clerical inhabitants from raids by native settlers.[15] While the Norse invasion had little impact in terms of the area settled, the Anglo-Normans who arrived in 1169 quickly conquered a large proportion of the country, leaving only Ulster and parts of the south and west unaffected. The period of the Anglo-Norman dominance was short and these new invaders were quickly assimilated into the ways of the older settlers. The Anglo-Normans also needed defended sites for their houses. Motte and bailey sites were their first type of defensive habitation and their distinctive earthen mounds can still be seen in many areas. The Anglo-Norman barons built large stone castles and smaller hall dwellings which were the homes of the minor landowners. As the Anglo-Norman settlement area was put under increased pressure a new type of more easily defended house was constructed. This was the tower house, a tall three or four storey stone house of which there are hundreds recorded.[16] Less is known about the homes of the older inhabitants in this period. After the coming of the Anglo-Normans there was a gradual abandoning of the raths, cashels and crannógs, although some continued to be occupied, especially in areas outside Anglo-Norman influence. These defended sites were replaced by houses on open sites and the two houses excavated at Calerguillamore, Co. Limerick, were probably typical of many houses of this period. Two roughly rectangular houses were discovered. The first measured 43 feet long by 20 feet wide and had a central hearth. The wall consisted of a stone foundation with clay and wattle walls. The second house, which was later in date measured 18 feet by 24 feet and also had a central hearth. These houses were occupied from the fourteenth to the sixteenth century, and the excavator properly drew attention to the similarity of these houses to houses of a post-medieval date in the same area.[17] Indeed at this date the progenitors of the typical Irish house are clearly recognizable.

Though the proof is inconclusive it seems certain that the entire indigenous population did not live in raths, hill forts and crannógs at any period. It has been argued that habitation sites beside undefended souterrains may have been the homes of a large proportion of the population.[18] Souterrains were underground passages and chambers and were used for storing food. They were usually un-defended, but they may have been used as places of refuge and were often lined with dry stone incorporating air ducts in their construction. Hut clusters existed during the first millennium AD and may have been the homes of the unfree members of society. Such hut clusters may also be the prototypes of the house clusters described as *clachans* which survive in some parts of Ireland to the present day. The whole fascinating question of settlement is too extensive to allow full treatment here, but it should be remarked that even if these hut clusters are 'proto-clachans' there is no smooth line of continuity between Dark Age clusters and nineteenth-century clach-ans.[19] Many clachans came into being as a result of political, economic and social changes of the seventeenth and eighteenth centuries. The theory of a servile class living relatively unaffected in clustered settlements through the centuries of con-quest, war and change appears to have some validity. *Betaghs* in Anglo-Norman areas were probably the unfree indigenous population. In terms of houses and settle-ment this group was separated geographically and socially from their Norman masters.

The process of urbanization begun by the Norsemen was continued by the Anglo-Normans and during the thirteenth century many small towns and villages grew around the manors. Many such settlements were walled, giving a distinctive appearance to the medieval town; others, consisting of one or two streets close to the manor house and church, were undefended and a large number of small villages in rural Ireland are clearly recognizable as medieval in origin.[20]

The next great period of change in rural Ireland came in the sixteenth and seventeenth centuries when plantation and colonization caused major changes in land ownership, with only one-fifth of the land being retained by the older settlers by 1700. The effect on settlement and housing was great. In the planted areas the isolated single farm became the norm and a clear division between the houses of the rich and the poor was established. In the west, where many of the dispossessed landowners were forced to flee, older settlement patterns survived and house clusters are still a common sight in this region.

The eighteenth century brought a measure of peace to Ireland. The country was enjoying an uneasy peace after two hundred years of periodic war and rebellion. Though the fighting stopped, some of the suffering with which the country is all too familiar continued and famine and periodic distress due to crop failures began to occur with ominous regularity. The most serious famine was in 1741 when an estimated 300,000 persons died[21] and in the second half of the century government intervention was necessary on a number of occasions to prevent a recurrence of this devastation. Yet despite this the country was relatively peaceful and the population was on the increase.[22] This increase was reflected in housing and from the hearth tax returns we get indications of the increase in the number of houses. In the forty years up to 1791 the number of houses in the country increased by more than 75 per cent and the greatest increase was in Connaught where the number of houses more than doubled. After 1791 the number of new houses continued to increase and by 1821 the number of houses in Connaught had again almost doubled. Between 1821 and 1841 the number of houses in the country increased enormously [23] and the census report of that year was the first to give a detailed breakdown of houses of different types. By 1841, 40 per cent of houses in the country were one-roomed cabins and a further 37 per cent had between two and four rooms (pl. 1). The greatest increase in housing had obviously taken place in the poorest house types and many contemporary accounts describe the poverty of these dwellings. When compared with excavated houses of earlier times these are smaller and perhaps less comfortable. A description written in 1823 give an impression of their squalor:

'The interior of an Irish cabin—you must let me make you acquainted with one, which will serve for many under my eye—that you may judge how impossible it is for the greater part of the population however willing they may be to obtain the reward held out for cleanliness—a room fifteen feet by nine, no window, no chimney, not even the sign of a fireplace, a mud floor sunk considerably below the level of the road by the side of which it stands, originally ill made and in this wet season covered by almost one foot of water, in one corner are a few lighted sods of turf which, while they afford but little warmth to the wretched group around them, fill the room with volumes of smoke.'

Rural housing conditions were made even more uncomfortable by the shortage of fuel in wet seasons when it was difficult to dry the peat for the fires. The presence of a manure heap outside the doors, which was a sight remarked upon by many travellers, completed the picture of these damp cold houses. The massive increase in the poorest type of house meant that many lived in appalling conditions in pre-famine Ireland.[24]

The effects of the great famine of 1845–50 on folk life are probably seen most clearly in the record of traditional housing. The census reports for 1841 and 1851 recorded house types before and after the great famine. In this decade increases in the number of the three larger house types were reported while a massive decrease for the poorest was recorded: 355,689 or 72 per cent of the poorest houses disappeared, which, allowing six persons per house, represents the homes of over two million people. There were two million chronically poor people who relied on charity to survive before the famine. Of the million or so who died in the great famine most were labourers deprived of food and aid at a time when those accustomed to supporting the poor were themselves distressed. The *bothán scóir*, as the poorest type of house has been called, was almost wiped out during the great famine and this most obvious material manifestation of the poor before 1845 is now unknown in the countryside.[25] The famine did not bring an end to poverty and indeed the 1881 census recorded that there were 155,675 mud cabins occupied by 227,379 families in the country. Housing projects in the last quarter of the nineteenth century organized by the Congested Districts Board, County Councils and the Department of the Gaeltacht helped to change the housing pattern in many of the poorer districts of rural Ireland, and houses built under these schemes are instantly recognizable because of their uniformity of plan and materials. For the more prosperous there has also been a turning away from traditional houses, and houses built in the last twenty-five years rarely follow traditional patterns. New houses are now more likely to be built to plans which can be found in use in many countries and which display few distinctively national features. For this reason the study of the Irish traditional house will shortly become a matter of historical and archaeological investigation rather than field recording of inhabited dwellings.

The typical Irish house we now know springs from this historical tradition (pl. 2). The apparent similarity of all such houses hides fascinating regional variations which have led people to examine these differences to see if, from studying them,

dates and cultural origins can be deduced. One feature which has been observed is
the bed outshot, which was a small rectangular projection on one of the side walls
of the house—a small annexe, into which a bed was fitted (pl. 3). It has been shown
that the bed outshot was found in houses in an area of the west and north including
the counties Mayo, Donegal, Sligo, Leitrim, Roscommon, Derry and parts of
Fermanagh, Tyrone, Antrim, Monaghan and Armagh.[26] Erixon, who examined
Irish houses in the 1930s, showed that bed alcoves of a similar type were found in
many European countries[27] and Lucas, using literary sources, has argued that the
bed outshot was possibly 'the truncated remnant of an annexe to the ancient Irish
house which was used as a store room for food.[28] McCourt meanwhile has suggested that this may be a residual derivative of the former side aisle of earlier
houses.[29] Whatever the origin of the bed outshot its regional distribution shows a
marked contrast in house types between what has been described as the highland
zone in the west and north and the remainder of the country. Excavation of
datable house sites may yet provide further clues to origins of this feature.

Houses combining cow byre and dwelling display a roughly similar west and
south-west distribution[30] (pl. 4). It was only in the western region of Connaught and
Munster that this custom survived in recent years, but in the last century such houses
were to be found in most areas outside Leinster. In these houses milch cows were
tethered to the end wall of the house furthest from the hearth, and an open drain
under their tails ran under one of the side walls of the house and led into a slurry
pit outside. In many such houses there were two doors facing one another with a
paved walk between them. McCourt has recorded more elaborate byre-type
dwellings in Donegal and Tyrone where, in houses built into a hillside, the byre
was at a lower level than the kitchen and a sleeping loft was built over the byre-
end.[31] Structures of a similar type are to be seen in east Clare and on Cape Clear.

Though this custom was remarked upon by nineteenth-century travellers who
suggested that it was a sign of a very primitive people, the practice of keeping
cows in the house with humans was common in many parts of Europe. Åke
Campbell, the Swedish ethologist who was the first to scientifically investigate
Irish house types, suggested that such houses were not an original Irish type house
and Danaher has suggested that such houses may date to the early medieval period.
The earliest literary references are from the seventeenth century although it is in the
western half of the country that such houses lasted longest, and so byre-type
dwellings are probably survivals of earlier types rather than new styles introduced
in the seventeenth century by planters. A recent publication has even suggested
that these may date back to prehistoric times.[32] The custom of keeping cows in the
dwelling house came to an end in the present century, and indeed where the cow,

pig and hen were all accommodated in the past now only the domestic pet is tolerated. Structural evidence of byre-type dwellings can still be seen. When the cows were removed, the byre-end of the house was converted into a bedroom and a wooden partition sometimes made from a dresser or other furniture was used to screen off this new accommodation. Until recently houses of this type could be seen on the islands of Inishbofin off the Galway coast and Cape Clear off the Cork coast, but in most places such houses have been abandoned and are now used as byres or store sheds. In the areas where these houses existed a second major feature of Irish traditional house was rarely found. That feature was the so-called jamb-wall which is found in the eastern half of Ireland, roughly east of a line from Derry to Cork.

In houses with jamb-walls the entrance door usually opens directly in to the hearth in the centre of the house.[33] This obviously caused problems of smoke in chimneys with poor draught and so a screen wall was built, usually with a small window in it to enable a person sitting by the fire to have a view of the door. This screen wall is the jamb-wall which distinguishes such houses as a separate type. The wall is usually built parallel to the outside wall and directly inside the door, forming a type of passage from which one can enter the kitchen or the bedroom. The entrance to the bedroom, or in some houses the parlour, usually has a door while the kitchen entrance is open. Of course the jamb-wall made it almost impossible to bring a cow into the house and so jamb-wall houses and houses in which cows were stalled at night occupy roughly complementary areas in Ireland. There has been little written on the origins of jamb-walls. The large wooden screens found in the baronial halls in English medieval houses may provide clues as to the origin of this feature. Jamb-wall entrances were known in Tudor England and had become a common feature of English houses by the eighteenth century.[34] This house type may therefore have been introduced originally to Ireland by Tudor planters and gradually spread to its present limits during the succeeding centuries. It is certainly true that many such houses were built during what was perhaps the last great spate of house building using traditional materials and patterns in the late nineteenth century.[35]

Another architectural feature which adds variety to the traditional house in Ireland is the wide range of types of roof and thatch. The timbers supporting the thatch were usually A-shaped couples which support purlins or lighter timber. A few heavy couples were used in the west while in the east a greater number of lighter couples was common. In the west couples sometimes ended with a collar rafter at the top and this gives a flattened appearance with no definite roof ridge.[36] Cruck trusses discovered in the north of Ireland are of types found in various parts of England, but as yet no examples of this type of roofing timber have been found in any of the southern counties.[37] Over the timbers in all houses are placed strips of scraws which serve both as insulation and as a base on to which the straw could be secured. The first layer of thatch was sewn to this by means of a thatching needle, often using hay rope, and the outer covering followed. On the western seaboard from Cork to Antrim the outer layer of thatch was secured by a network of hay ropes closely spaced and either weighted at their ends with stones, or fastened to pegs driven into the outer walls of the house.[38] On Cape Clear Island projecting stones on the gable walls gave easy access to the roof and made the thatchers' work easier (pl. 6). Somewhat similar features have been recorded on Lewis in the western isles of Scotland.[39] In other areas the usual method of thatching was to use sally, hazel bog fir or briar rods as pins, usually called *scollops*, to hold handfuls of thatch in place on the roof. Mud, to secure thatch, was also used. The outer covering was usually of wheaten or barley straw, though rye straw was also highly praised. In parts of Munster rushes, lake and river reed (pl. 9) were used, as was flax thatch in some northern countries. Older accounts also describe how unlikely materials like heather, bracken, potato stalks and bent grass were used.[40] The end product in the construction of such roofs presents a wide variety of shapes and designs. In the areas where scollops are used it is common to find bobbins at the ridge. Bobbins were tightly bound twists of straw arranged in rows on hazel sticks. When the thatching was complete these presented a decorative line at the top (pl. 5). It was also the custom in certain areas to add a decorative lattice work of rods near the ridge or near the eaves. These rods were usually the only ones to be seen and they gave added protection against wind, the great enemy of thatch, at the most sensitive points. Another variation in roof types was between hipped and stepped gables. Hipped gables are usually found in the same areas as jamb-walls while the stepped gables are found in the western parts of the country especially where rope-thatch is common. The lines of division are not clear, however, and in Co. Offaly in the midlands the occasional straight gable without the distinctive ladder-like steps is found side by side with a larger number of hip gables. It is interesting to speculate how this happens; it probably represents the mixed cultural influences of the area, where planters and older inhabitants co-existed from the mid sixteenth century.

Finally it must be noted that roofing materials were almost always those which could be obtained locally and roofs were usually built by the occupiers. Thatchers only became a specialized group as society became more sophisticated and affluent. The timber used in older houses was often crude and unplaned, and the wood in the couples was almost invariably fastened with wooden pegs.

In all Irish houses the fire was the centre of activity and the most important part of the house. In the earliest houses the hearth was in the middle of the floor and the smoke escaped through a smoke hole in the roof. In houses which survived into the modern period the hearth was always on the main axis of the house, either on

*Fig. 2. Fireplace of Co. Kerry house.*

the gable wall, in the case of byre-type houses, or in the centre in the jamb-wall type. Many of the old chimneys were sturdily constructed of dressed stone, but the majority appear to have a type of chimney hood of clay-plastered wickerwork or of lath and plaster; a heavy beam supported this hood. The end of the beam occasionally rested on the front and rear walls of the house and the front of the wickerwork hood rested on this beam. In jamb-wall houses the beam sometimes ended at the jamb-wall, while in some areas the chimney hood rested on two timber uprights, one on either side of the fire. The partitioned hearth has a wider distribution than the jamb-wall. As chimney flues were more constricted in the nineteenth century it became the practice to have small lofts on each side in front of the chimney and still supported by the heavy beam which in coastal areas, in the days of wooden ships, was often made from driftwood. Such lofts were common in Fermanagh, Mayo and Armagh where they were used for storage or as additional sleeping accommodation.[41] In Mayo two little poles projected horizontally over the fire-place, and these formed a loft between them which was made of wattles with a straw mat spread on top. Barley grain, which was pulled off straw with the fingers, was put up on this loft to dry and left there for a long time. When dry it was pounded, often with a spade in a barrel to remove chaff. Afterwards it was winnowed and the grain used for potheen-making.[42] Barley was also dried on two sheets suspended from rafters. In the south and west, lofts for beds were usually at the other end of the kitchen and in both cases access was by stairs usually resembling a steep ship's ladder. Another variation of the wickerwork hood was a three-sided canopy secured to the wall which formed the fourth side of the flue. Wicker chimneys can now be easily identified in deserted houses, but formerly, when the house was occupied, it was difficult to know what method of construction was used, as whitewash made chimneys and walls look alike. The best indication was the chimney stack, which was often made of wickerwork or timber and in some cases the thatch almost completely covered this feature (pl. 14). The hearth, as so many writers have properly observed, was the focal point of the house. In draughty houses the only truly warm place was near the fire (pl. 11) and there the families' meals were cooked and often eaten. The fire in the evenings was also the principal source of light and the place where stories were told and entertainment was to be had. Little wonder that so many books of popular literature included the word fire-side in their titles.[43] The very word conveyed the idea of warmth, comfort and hospitality.

The materials used to build the various houses were largely determined by the availability of stone, mud or brick locally. Stone houses were found in most areas but principally in mountainous districts. Mud walls were common in Leinster and were also found, where stone was scarce, in the other three provinces. Sod houses were also built, usually for the poor, and were often erected in one day for evicted tenants in the last century.[44] Brick-making was a local industry, especially along the canals in the last century, though brick houses in rural Ireland are usually associated with the activities of reforming or improving landlords.[45]

Floors were usually of beaten earth, or daub, as it is commonly called. Stone flags were greatly favoured and even the poorest houses had stone flags around the hearth. Windows in the older houses were almost invariably small and few to reduce the amount paid in the infamous window-tax, called 'typhus-tax' by its opponents, who argued that lack of ventilation had disastrous consequences. Glass was a luxury and dried sheepskins were used at night to block window apertures, as were sods of turf and wickerwork; even the use of a mare's placenta has been recorded.[46] This tax was withdrawn in the nineteenth century but the habit, born out of necessity, of leaving the door open to give light was well established. Half doors are yet another feature of Irish houses, and effectively convert the door aperture into a sort of window opening (pl. 14). A curious survival until recent times of a feature of ancient Irish houses was the use of wattle and straw mat doors in primitive houses. The scarcity of timber as well as continuous tradition encouraged the use of such materials.[47] Straw was also used to line the roof under the thatch in Co. Waterford and reed roof lining was recorded in Co. Limerick.[48] Ceilings in many houses were of board in recent years and in poorer houses sacking was used as a foundation and a skimming of 'plaster and wash' was applied to this. A house at Shantallow, Co. Derry, had a ceiling lined with 'plaited strips of marram grass sewn together and secured to the purlins by handmade nails'.[49] In Co. Dublin straw matting was used as a ceiling in circular horse walks. The expertise in handling straw, grasses and wattle is seen repeatedly in different aspects of material folk culture in Ireland.

Finally it must be mentioned that there are many folk beliefs about houses. The site on which a house was built in rural Ireland was always chosen with consideration not just for the physical position but also with a view to avoiding fairy paths and other unlucky locations.[50] In the midlands oral tradition tells of many houses accidentally built on such locations. If this happened front and rear doors had to be left open continuously and a container of water constantly full had to be kept in the house to appease the disturbed travellers. For those who shut the doors progressively more serious disturbances took place until the house became uninhabitable. Ó'Suilleabháin has described the foundation sacrifices which were commonly used to ensure the luck of the new house. Eggs, playing cards, candles, vegetables, wine, newspapers, tobacco, iron, horseshoes, whiskey and clay from a holy place were all used in different areas as charms against misfortune.[51] Among a deeply religious people, such practices still continued, as in Offaly, side by side with the placing of St Benedict medals in the four corners of the house. Foundation sacrifices are known from almost all types of house site in Ireland from earliest times. Human skulls were discovered at Ballinderry crannóg. Tradition says that St Columcille's brother Dobhran was buried alive to placate the spirits before a church could be built in Iona[52] and there is a tradition in modern times of burying live animals in

Co. Westmeath.[53] There seems little doubt that animal sacrifice replaced human sacrifice in yet another example of the continuity of folk custom and tradition in Ireland.[54]

Of all the foundation sacrifices undoubtedly that of burying horses and cows skulls was the most widespread. This custom was recorded in many areas. In the townland of Mucknanstown on the Dublin–Meath border, horses' skulls were buried under the floors of many houses and in one case up to ten skulls were found under the floor of one room. Though, in the modern period, such skulls were occasionally placed to make floorboards give a resonant sound either for dancers or singers, yet the sacrifical significance of such burials was probably more important in an earlier age when the horse at least was regarded as a sacred animal in Ireland.

In some northern countries yet another custom connected with house building has been recorded. This is the custom of erecting a flag or a substitute for one when the building of a new house has reached the chimney stage. The purpose was supposed to be to remind the owner that some incentives would speed the completion of the work. This custom was widely established in Co. Down from where it appears to have spread to Antrim, Derry and westwards to Fermanagh. Gailey, who recorded this international custom in Ulster, concluded that this is of fairly recent origin in Ireland.[55]

Houses in rural Ireland today are far different from what was the norm in 1950. People no longer choose to live in traditional houses and abandon them as quickly as possible or so alter and extend them as to make them unrecognizable as traditional houses. Few people can resist tearing down these old houses and erecting in their place bungalows of international design, often prefabricated, which are completely out of sympathy with the surroundings. Writing about houses in the western isands of Scotland Hammond Innes wrote:

'These compact, neat thatched homesteads that fit so snugly into their background are infinitely more suited to the island life than the wretched little jerrybuilt houses that now clutter the landscape, architectural excrescences that are too often cracked and damp and draughty.'[56]

These comments apply to Ireland also. One hopeful sign, however, has been the erection of traditional houses with all modern conveniences as holiday homes for tourists. The striking popularity of these may cause a fresh realization of the architectural beauty of our traditional houses.

# 2 Furniture

Unlike houses, furniture in rural Ireland has attracted little attention. As with costume no distinctive style of peasant furniture evolved in Ireland. The earliest furniture was of a fundamental kind catering for a man's needs when sitting, sleeping, eating and cooking. Few articles of furniture are highly decorated and houses traditionally contained few ornaments; such ornaments that were found usually had religious significance and were prized or valued for this rather than for their visual impact. Highly decorative St Brighid's Crosses were found in every area and indeed in some areas it was the custom to fix a new one to the inside of the thatch every year on 1st February (pl. 137). In such houses it was possible to tell the age of the house from the number of crosses on the ceiling.[1] In the early nineteenth century travelling pedlars sold prints with religious themes and many examples of their wares are still to be seen in rural houses. These prints, however, are of a type found in every western European country and are not distinctively Irish. Although no distinctive peasant furniture evolved, a number of pieces like settle beds, dressers, bins and chairs of a particular type are recognized as belonging to traditional houses in rural Ireland. Most of these are functional and made from materials easily obtainable by country folk. Many pieces ultimately derive from continental European sources but, as Gailey has suggested, their arrangement about the kitchen was probably influenced by an older Atlantic-fringe tradition which may even pre-date the Gaelic tradition on these islands.[2]

From the limited sources available it is difficult to present a satisfactory account of the evolution of particular articles of furniture. We know little about the sleeping arrangements in prehistoric Ireland, but it can be assumed from the size of the houses that the sleeping accommodation was shared by the entire family. This tradition continued until at least the nineteenth century in rural Ireland.

In the early historic period (c. AD 800–1200) wooden beds with straw and rushes were common and the great Irish cloaks acted as blankets. Little innovation probably took place in sleeping arrangement in the first thousand years of the historic period. In a society which had few possessions people probably slept either in rough wooden beds or on mats on the floors of houses. The planters of the Tudor and Stuart period probably introduced the settle bed, which is also known as a 'press bed' or a 'saddle bed'. Settle beds are designed in such a way that they can be used during the day as a seat and at night time can be opened out to provide a bed (fig. 3). This bed was very popular in rural Ireland and until recent times could be

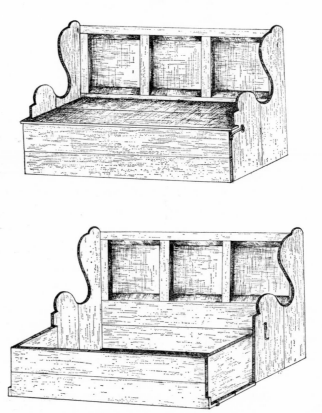

*Fig. 3. Settle bed, Montiagh, Co. Galway. This could be shut as a seat and open as a bed.*

found in houses in all districts. Though northern examples are usually almost 6 feet long, many examples from other areas are much shorter and the occupants must have been forced to sleep in a crouched position.[3] Settle beds display many local variations and most of them are among the most attractive pieces of furniture found in traditional houses in recent years.

 The introduction of settle beds did not immediately alter sleeping habits. Dunton in the seventeenth century described sleeping in large, soft, white bundles

*1. Irish houses, c. 1840. After Hall.*

*2. Farmhouse, Moville, Co. Donegal (B.F. TY121).*

*3. House with bed outshot, Croagh Patrick, Co. Mayo (N.L.I. 1267WL).*

4. *Deserted house combining byre and dwelling, Cape Clear, Co. Cork.*

5. *Hip-roofed house with bobbins at ridge, Co. Meath.*

6. *Projecting stones on gable of house, Cape Clear, Co. Cork.*

7. *Rope-thatch tied to pegs, Teelin, Co. Donegal* (B.F. TY204).

8. *Rope-thatch tied to poles and pegs, Barnes Gap, Co. Donegal* (N.L.I. Imp. 1556).

9. *Below right: Rope-thatch weighed down with stones, Keel Bay, Co. Mayo* (N.L.I. 1287WL).

10. *River reed stacked for thatching* (N.M.I. DF452).

*11. House interior (N.L.I. 3554WL).*

*12. Half-door, Connemara, Co. Galway (B.F. TY35).*

*13. Bed beside fireplace, Mrs Annie McCrae, Teebane East, Co. Tyrone (N.M.I. DF304).*

*14. Timber chimney top, Caddelbrook, Co. Roscommon (N.M.I. DF348).*

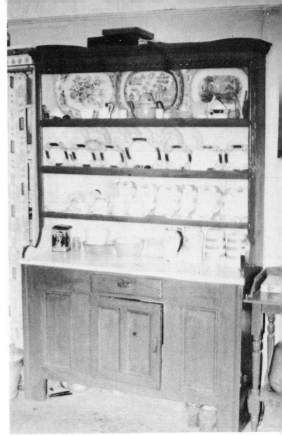

15. *Dresser, Belmont, Co. Offaly.*

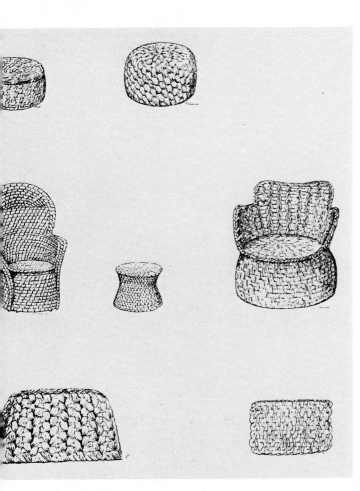

16. *Straw objects: two round seats, Doolin, Co. Clare, and Killeenaran, Co. Galway; chair, Gardamus, Co. Wexford; seat, Tuam, Co. Galway, and chair, Cape Clear, Co. Cork; two straw mats, Co. Galway* (N.M.I. EF11).

17. *Wicker cradle, Inishere, Co. Galway* (N.M.I. EF361).

*18. Knife and spoon box, Teebane,*
*Co. Tyrone (N.M.I. DF301).*

*19. Stave-built wooden noggin, Co. Cavan*
*(N.M.I. EF179).*

*20. Kneading trough, Co. Limerick*
*(N.M.I. EF103).*

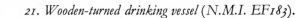

*21. Wooden-turned drinking vessel (N.M.I. EF183).*

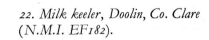

*22. Milk keeler, Doolin, Co. Clare (N.M.I. EF182).*

*23. Roasting spit, Dunlavin, Co. Wicklow (N.M.I. EF151).*

24. *Crusie lamps* (N.M.I. CF12).

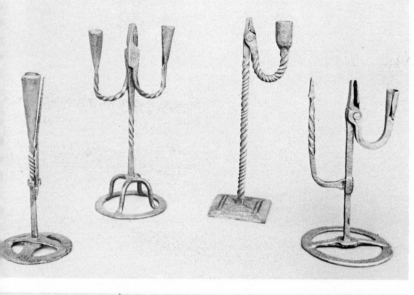

25. *Rush and candle holders, Tuam, Co. Galway, Virginia, Co. Cavan, Garadine, Co. Meath, and Co. Waterford* (N.M.I. EF72).

26. *Two tin candle lanterns* (N.M.I. CF11).

of woollen breadeen laid on rushes,[4] and a poem of the same period shows that
communal sleeping was still the norm:

> *Under a plad which did extend*
> *Cross the whole floor from end to end,*
> *On litter laid, like horse at manger*
> *Which served for family and stranger.*[5]

Sleeping 'in stradogue', as the habit of communal sleeping was known in the
west, continued down to the present century.[6] Otway described this in Co. Mayo
in the nineteenth century:

'The floor is thickly strewn with fresh rushes, and stripping themselves entirely,
the whole family lie down at once together, covering themselves with blankets, if
they have them, if not, with their day clothing, but they lie decently, and in order;
the eldest daughter next to the wall farthest from the door, then all the sisters,
according to their ages; next the mother, father and sons in succession and then
the strangers, whether the travelling pedlar, or tailor or beggar.'[7]

In Donegal the whole family slept in one bed known from the eighteenth century
to the twentieth century as a 'thorough bed'.[8] Undoubtedly in certain areas and
among certain classes the habit of sleeping on the floor lasted until recent times.
Where this occurred the family usually slept in front of the fire in the centre of the
house which was probably the only vacant space in such cramped accommodation.

As already mentioned, one type of house had in its structural design a space left
for a bed. This was the bed outshot which was found in the north-west and was
described in the early nineteenth century as 'a little recess called a "hag"' which is
made into the side wall of the house opposite the family fire, for one bed; this is
divided from the fire and from the body of the house by straw mats, which hang
parallel with the wall from the roof by way of a curtain.[9] In later years the straw
mats gave way to curtains as the photographs show (pl. 13). The actual bed in the
outshot was usually made of timber, sometimes with a rope base made from twisted
bog fir.[10] This bed was usually for the father and mother while children and
strangers slept elsewhere. There is, of course, plenty of evidence of beds being
used by the indigenous population in modern times. The Earl of Tyrone when he
fled the country in 1607 left behind him 'an old bedstead'[11] and Otway recorded in
the early nineteenth century that in two-roomed houses in Mayo 'truckles' were
used to raise beds and bedding from damp floors.[12] Gradually beds came into
general use and Gailey has identified four types of traditional kitchen beds in rural
Ireland. These were the settle, outshot, box and tester beds.[13] The box bed was a

c

timber bed with canopy and closed sides sometimes with hinged doors. Such beds were known in Wexford as 'covered car' beds[14] because of their similarity, while in neighbouring Waterford there is a traditional connection between the construction of such beds and horses' carts.[15] Timber parts of these beds were used occasionally for other purposes. Box beds were recorded in many areas in Ulster, and

*Fig. 4. Tester bed, Benvoran, Co. Clare.*

are known in parts of the south-east and south-west. Field recording of this item is not satisfactory and consequently little is known of this bed type in the south. Further recording may reveal more about box beds, but there is evidence to suggest that these are of fairly recent origin because of the known distribution pattern. The tester bed, on the other hand, was probably introduced at an earlier date as its distribution in all areas is much wider. Tester beds are basically beds with a canopy overhead and were found in the bed outshot as well as in kitchens, bedrooms and lofts.[16] They were copied from the more elaborate examples found in the houses of the rich, and became very popular.

Other types of bed were also used, but they have long since disappeared. Hall recorded seeing wicker beds like cradles big enough for two grown people in use in Limerick in 1831[17] (pl. 17). The bedding for all types of bed varied. Straw mats, rushes, bennet, ferns, chaff, down and feathers of both domestic and wild birds are often mentioned. Straw mattresses were perhaps the most popular and, though rarely seen now, door mats of similar construction are often seen in Co. Offaly.

Predictably, beliefs about various types of beds were widespread. In west Cork it is believed that beds should lie along a house but not across it,[18] while in Longford custom dictated that the head of the bed should never face west.[19] Straw mattresses were regarded in Co. Wexford as being superior to feather beds, which were supposed to leave a man fatigued in the morning. In Co. Waterford it was believed that sleeping on rush beds kept one healthy and indeed it was rush beds which gave Ireland's mythological heroes, the Fianna, their health and strength.[20] Because the Saviour slept in a bed of green rushes it was said in the Decies that no one ever felt cold on such a bed,[21] while at the opposite end of the country in Donegal a bed of black sedge was greatly prized for the same reason.[22] One custom which has been widely recorded is that of taking a dying person from the bed and placing him on a bundle of straw, called a 'shake down', on the floor. One account of this habit links it to the danger of contagion in cases of fever deaths, and indeed the frequent admonitions to burn the beds of fever victims may have helped to establish this custom.[23] Similarly, publications and proclamations by Boards of Health led to the enormous popularity of lime as whitewash for both inside and outside rural houses. As with all aspects of life and tradition in rural Ireland, religious custom was followed when new beds were brought to a house or even when straw was changed in old beds. In Co. Mayo a wisp of straw was lighted and the sign of the cross was made with this over the new bedding.[24]

In the present century new types of mattresses became popular. Most harness makers, and there were many of them, had hair teasing machines and many people had mattresses made up of horse hair and other materials. The harness maker found for a period that his trade was expanding as he became an upholsterer as well, but the introduction of spring mattresses and the decline of the horse as a working animal cut short his brief period of prosperity.

Seats in traditional houses were scarce. As the hearth was the centre of all activities seats were usually found around it, but as space was confined it is rare to find traditional houses with large chairs. The settle bed could be used as a seat during the day time and in some places a bench seat of a similar size and shape was sometimes found. Stools were more common, however, and another aspect of domestic architecture influenced all types of seat: the absence of proper chimney canopies in early houses meant that many houses were very smoky so for comfort the lower the seat was the better. Consequently most stools and chairs had very short legs—the seats often no more than 10 inches off the floor. Pococke, who toured Ireland, described how he was glad to take a low seat by the fire to avoid smoke.[25] Few descriptions of seats can be given for the period before 1800. Hall described seeing wicker seats in Limerick and Kerry in the early nineteenth century.[26] The seats which survived into living memory probably tell us as much about seating in past centuries as we are likely to learn from literary sources. Around the hearth in many houses seats were built into the hob. Sods of turf were used as stools, but small stools made of timber or straw were common all over Ireland. Three-legged wooden stools were used everywhere and were often known as 'creepies'. Straw stools were called 'bosses' in Wexford, Clare and Donegal. Surviving examples are made both of plaited straw and of straw bound into rolls with brambles (pl. 16). This latter craft is sometimes known as lip work[27] and was a full-time occupation for some in nineteenth-century Wexford.[28] Full armchairs were also constructed of straw and three-legged chairs with narrow backs made by extending one leg are also found. Suggan chairs with wooden frames and seats made from twisted straw rope were also popular, but chairs tended in the main to be plain, functional, small and few. The seat of honour in rural Ireland was not determined by its size or make but by its position. Proximity to the fire was the determining factor and the seats of honour, usually reserved for the woman and the man of the house, were those on either side of the fire. From old photographs it can be seen that small chairs with holes in the seats were fashioned for children.

Meal-bins were to be found in most rural houses and in these the family's supply of grain was stored. These bins were made of wood with a sloping lid, and often divided into two compartments which in recent years were filled with oatmeal and flour respectively.[29] Meal-bins enabled people to store oatmeal in clean, dry conditions: it was packed tightly into the bin to keep it from the air as much as possible and this prevented it becoming sour. To pack the oatmeal tightly the practice in Ireland was to get children to stand or tramp on it; a similar procedure was followed in Wales.[30] Chests of various kinds were common before the introduction of wardrobes, and often a bride brought with her to her new home a chest full of linen, frieze, thread, wool, blankets and other valuables as part of her dowry. This is not surprising when it is remembered that traditionally wedding presents supplied all household furniture needs except a bed and a table.[31] Sometimes rolls of fabric were passed on as heirlooms for two generations without being used. Presses and wardrobes gradually replaced chests, which became associated primarily with emigrants.

The most striking piece of furniture in traditional rural houses was the kitchen dresser (pl. 15). Dressers of various kinds are to be found, but the feature common to all is that they have an upper section usually consisting of two or three shelves

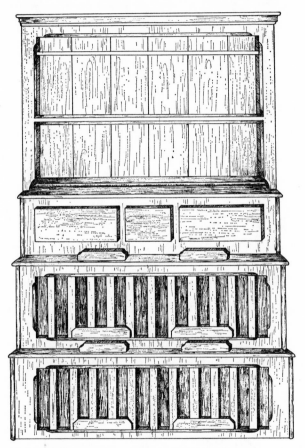

*Fig. 5. Dresser, Bohermore, Co. Limerick.*

on which dishes and plates are rested. On the fronts of the shelves cups are suspended from hooks. The lower section of the dresser is usually deeper, and the top often forms a 'work top' for cutting bread and other small domestic tasks. The bottom section of the dresser is usually a cupboard in modern examples, but in older types the bottom section was often open and water pails or milking vessels were stored there. In some older examples in the hatching season a sitting hen or goose was frequently given safe and warm accommodation there (fig. 5).

Dressers were probably copied from the type of furniture found in medieval castles[32] but did not become popular in rural houses until the eighteenth century.[33] They became very popular in the nineteenth century, possibly because of both their utilitarian value and their beauty, for wares and food could be stored and the family's best ware could be displayed to every visitor. Many of the poor could not afford dressers, however, and in many older houses the 'ware rack' or 'tin rail' is still seen. This item consists of a wooden framework usually with three upright and three horizontal laths morticed together into which hooks were screwed. In earlier days this was sufficient to carry all the delft or tin ware which a family possessed. Such racks and shelves of various kinds were probably the forerunners of dressers, and cutlery, which in modern times has been kept in a knife drawer in the lower part of the dresser or under the scrubbed table, was formerly kept in a specially designed knife box. This usually consisted of a board which was attached to the wall with a small box at the lower end (pl. 18). A similar box was sometimes used to hold salt, which was a valuable commodity in the past. Tobacco, tea and other delicate valuables were often stored in safe, dry wall holes around the hearth.

The extent to which ware and vessels of various types were available to the rural population in Ireland in different periods is a matter of conjecture. In the middle of a period of agrarian outrage in the eighteenth century the gentlemen Whiteboys were warned that the common Whiteboys:

'May one night pass a resolution that plated work looks as well as solid silver on a side-board, and vote it highly *unconstitutional and a grievance*, that you should have silver cups to drink good beer and cyder, and silver spoons to sup rich soups with, whilst they are obliged to drink sour milk out of wooden piggins, and eat stir-about with shells, or pewter, or horn spoons.'[34]

For the majority of the rural population in the period before 1800 wooden platters, cups and spoons as well as shells and horn spoons were widely used (pls. 19–22). Pococke described how sea shells were used for everything in Erris, how whiskey was served in eggshells and how all the vessels were of wood.[35] Derricke in the late sixteenth century presented a similar view of the native Irish:

*Their platters are of wood,*
*By cunning turners made.*
*But not of pewter (credit me)*
*As is our English trade.*[36]

The absence of metal is remarked upon by many travellers and this is surprising considering the magnificent metal cauldrons which were in use in the Bronze Age in Ireland. Yet no metal cauldrons which could be dated to the Early Christian period[37] have been discovered, and it must be assumed that large metal cooking pots were unknown in Ireland at this time. Pottery vessels were in use in Ireland from at least the Neolithic period, but in the early Christian period native pottery was found mainly in a small area in the north-east. For cooking purposes it is unlikely that pottery vessels were widely used.[38] The Normans introduced new pottery and potters to Ireland and from the thirteenth century brass pots and skillets began to appear in the towns and presumably in the houses of the rich.[39] From the sixteenth century a new type of brass pot made its appearance, and from the beginning of the seventeenth century iron vessels began to be used.[40] By the beginning of the nineteenth century iron pot ovens and pots of various sizes had replaced brass in importance, and had become a common feature in the houses of both rich and poor alike. Pewter and brass cooking vessels, which had been very valuable in the late medieval period, gradually decreased in value until by the late eighteenth century the common Whiteboys could include pewter in their lists of possessions without admitting to any great wealth.

In the absence of metal vessels in which food could be boiled directly over a fire, it is obvious that other methods of cooking had to be attempted. In some areas stones heated in fires were put into water in wooden lined pits and in this way the water could be boiled and presumably meat cooked. Sites where this operation took place have been excavated, and such sites known as *fulacht fiadh* have been given dates from the Bronze Age to perhaps the early Christian era or later.[41] Meat was also boiled in cow-hide bags as Derricke's woodcut of the sixteenth century illustrates (fig. 6). The tradition of boiling liquids using heated stone continued into this century as a teacher from Cruit Island, Co. Donegal, recorded that he often drank milk heated in this way.[42] While boiling obviously presented difficulties, the use of spits for roasting was widespread, as can be seen from the numbers mentioned in wills and inventories[43] (pl. 23).

Wooden vessels were the norm in the majority of houses in rural Ireland up to 1800 and in many areas for long afterwards. These vessels were made either by carving them out laboriously from a single piece of wood or by turning them on a pole lathe. Alternatively, vessels could be built up using staves in a manner similar to the way a cooper builds a barrel.[44] These rarely had metal hoops but often had interlocking thick bands of timber. Vessels of all of these types were found in almost every period and many of them display considerable craftsmanship. Knowledge of how to use horn, a raw material for spoons and other smaller articles of domestic use, was also widespread. Medieval horn combs have been

*Fig. 6. Irish chieftain's feast, 1581. After Derricke.*

excavated in Dublin, and a tradition of making similar type fine-toothed combs persisted in Connemara until the present century.[45]

Delft ware was made in Ireland from the eighteenth century and gradually both Irish and foreign-made ware of this type became popular in rural Ireland.[46] Some local potters made earthenware crocks, bowls, jugs and jars.[47] By 1900 most houses in rural Ireland had a dresser displaying a range of mugs, plates and dishes, as well as large crocks or coolers in which milk was allowed to set so that cream could be skimmed off for churning to make butter. Itinerant salesmen, sometimes tinkers, carried ware to fairs and to houses in remote districts. 'Willow pattern' was the most popular type of design, followed closely by a design called 'Asiatic pheasant'. In later years jugs large enough to hold about a pint or two became popular and many jam manufacturers sold their produce in such containers. Pottery ware of various kinds was expensive and so its spread to poorer areas was slow. An indication of its value can be gauged from the fact that plates and other items were not discarded when broken, but were kept until the tinker called and repaired them.[48] This he did by drilling small holes on either side of the break and lacing the pieces together again by means of wire and tin. Though probably unhygienic, such repairs made the vessels serviceable again.

Selling and repairing pottery vessels of various types was not the tinker's main role in rural Ireland. It was as tinsmiths they were best known. It is impossible to say when tinkers became a separate identifiable social group, for although tinkers are mentioned as early as 1175, they were then merely a group of craft workers. As recently as 1865 they were not easily identifiable in their social behaviour from many of the ordinary population. In the mid nineteenth century their craft was their sole distinguishing feature. In the past hundred years, however, they have become clearly identifiable as a group in Irish society which still remains nomadic and as such are even further removed from society in general. In the nineteenth century the tinker, or traveller as people prefer to call him now, was a useful member of society. He provided tin ware of various sizes and shapes which was

*Fig. 7. Potatoes served in traditional manner.*

eagerly sought by country people for both domestic and farm use. The itinerant tinsmith also repaired his ware, and it was only the availability of cheap plastic containers that finally killed the tinsmith's trade in rural Ireland in the last two decades.[49]

In traditional Irish houses tables are of comparatively recent origin. Until well into this century many houses in poor and remote districts contained none, and at meal times the family sat around the fire and ate from a basket set on top of a three-legged iron pot[50] (fig. 7). Where tables were found they were rarely moved out from the side wall and tables do not feature in many customs or traditions. In earlier periods small boards were sometimes used as tables and hung on the wall when not in use.[51] From such tables developed the table hinged to the wall which could be stored flat against the wall because of its collapsible leg or legs. Gailey has recorded such tables in many parts of south Ulster,[52] and similar tables were found in Wexford, Carlow, Cork and Kerry.[53] In the present century a low solid oak table became popular in many houses and this in most areas was unpainted. The tops of these tables were scrubbed regularly so that they often stood in marked contrast to the other items of furniture which were often painted and repainted.[54]

Baskets were used for many purposes in Irish houses. Baskets used as tables have already been mentioned and in many areas the whole family sat around a flat basket of potatoes, perhaps with herring in the centre, and all ate from this common wickerwork vessel.[55] Baskets were also used as containers for turf or raw potatoes; inverted, a basket could become a seat, and the quick-growing osier could also be twisted to make a muzzle for any animal. Most houses had a special 'sally garden' and local names abound for different types of basket as the following short account from Cape Clear demonstrates:

'A "rishawn" was made of them (osiers) and that was the only table they had for potatoes. "Sheehogues" also, and these were used for picking potatoes from the ridges at harvest time. "Kleevawns" and "sharragawns", both commoner baskets used for general purposes, were also made from the osier twigs. And, finally, pots or creels with wooden bottoms were made out of them in order to hold top-loads on a horse or donkey, for there were no butts then or any thought of them.'[56]

From bed to chimney hood, from egg basket to toy rattle, the ubiquitous osier found many uses in the traditional Irish house.

Light is another of man's basic needs, and in common with many European countries the crusie lamp is perhaps the most primitive type of lamp found in Ireland. Crusie lamps consist of a pear-shaped pan, usually of iron, which was filled with oil. The oil used in the coastal regions of Northern Ireland, where the best examples are found, was usually fish oil, though the use of tallow, lard, vegetable oils and even butter has also been recorded. The wick was generally made from a piece of twisted cloth laid along the spout or lip. Many of the lamps which survive have two pans—the lower one being slightly larger than the upper but of the same shape (pl. 24). The lower pan is designed to catch any oil which has dripped from the wick. From the back of the lower or drip pan there rose a strap of metal which was usually joined by a swivel to a hook or a spike. In this way the lamp could be either hung or driven into a wall. The upper pan, containing the fuel, was hung on a notched rack projecting from the strap and this enabled it to be hung at different angles to ensure that the oil constantly fed the wick. Crusie lamps of various types were in widespread use in Ireland from prehistoric times to the end of the last century, when they were found principally on the northern coast. More primitive examples made from shells were recorded in Aran and in Co. Kerry. Describing how such lamps were used on Cape Clear, Conchúr Ó'Síocháin wrote:

'They used to take the livers from hake or cod to that end (i.e. to get oil), and put them all together in a big, capacious vat or in a spacious open tub. To cure them then for the special purpose they first shook a handful of salt over them; after that the container was left in the open air for the sun to draw the oil out of the livers. This was skimmed by using a large shell and was put in a jar or bottles which were well corked. There was a special appliance for burning it—that is a *slige* or creuset. The oil was poured into it and whittled rushes were used as wicks. If the woman of the house wanted to go into any corner of the house she would dip a rush in the oil, light it and take it with her in her hand. That was the kind of light they had at the time, it was a poor, dim thing indeed.'[57]

Rushes dipped in oil were widely used. The rushes were gathered in the late summer and peeled, leaving one or two strips to hold the pith together. After drying in the sun they were dipped in melted fat. Sometimes a special vessel called a grisset was used to melt the fat and dip the rushes. Holders for rushlights were found in most districts. Many holders were designed to hold both rushlights and candles, which in Ireland were usually made from tallow. The commonest type of rushlight holder consisted of a device like tongs to hold the rush (pl. 25). One jaw of this was fixed and usually formed by the upper end of the shaft of the holder. The other jaw was movable and was kept pressed against the rush by having its outer end elongated, bent outwards and weighted either with a knob of metal or with a candle socket. In other examples the jaws were closed by a spring and where no tongs were used the rush was held either in a clip alongside the candle socket or in a notch in a metal arm. These were usually made by a local blacksmith, and many are excellent examples of craftsmanship. When in use they stood on a table or on a shelf, while some were designed to stand on the floor. Others were designed to fit on to a loom and some are provided with an attachment for raising and lowering the light.[58] Rushlights were widely used in Ireland from at least the seventeenth century, and the simplest holder was probably a cleft stick driven into a sod of peat.[59] Tallow candles were made in special moulds. In the present century paraffin replaced fish oil and fat, and commercially produced oil-lamps became common. The Electricity Supply Board, set up in 1927, began at a later period to plan rural electrification and this scheme to bring electricity to country areas ended in 1975 with most areas by then linked to the national service. Crusies, rushlights and oil lamps are now eagerly sought antiques rather than essential objects for everyday use (pl. 26).

This description of furniture and plenishings refers only to what could be seen in ordinary houses in rural Ireland. In the houses of the more prosperous, furniture appliances and ware purchased in the towns and cities could be seen. Tilley lamps were popular in larger houses before the introduction of electricity. The parlour was a feature of many three-roomed houses in rural Ireland, and here the best pieces were placed almost for display purposes. The parlour table usually dominated the room and sometimes a gramophone was installed. Family portrait photographs became popular at the end of the last century and, in common with people in many lands, china dogs, geraniums and lace curtains conveyed a feeling of respectability much sought after by people in rural Ireland.[60]

Until the present century goods found in Irish rural houses tended to be simple and functional. The wills which had to be registered in the medieval period in areas under Norman rule demonstrate this. Very often the most valuable items even for town dwellers were pots, pans, beds and chairs. In 1477 one will included twenty 'couples' (roof timbers) sown in the fields, each worth five shillings, and these were among the most valued possessions of the deceased.[61]

Building timbers from the fifteenth to the nineteenth century remained valuable possessions,[62] and evicted tenants in the nineteenth century were occasionally allowed to take their roof timbers with them. When Rory Óg Ó'Moore baited his ill-fated trap for Sir Barnaby Fitzpatrick in the 1570s he let it be known that his band would have with them 'pots, pans, pewter, nappery, linen and other household stuff and implements'.[63] An inventory of the goods left by the Earl of Tyrone after his sudden flight to Spain in 1607 shows how little even the most powerful Irish chief had. The list compiled by Sir Toby Caulfield included:

'2 long tables, 2 long forms, an old bedstead, an old trunk, a long stool, 8 hogs-heads, $\frac{1}{2}$ cwt of hops, 3 hogsheads of salt, a silk jacket, 8 vessels of butter containing $4\frac{1}{2}$ barrels, 2 iron spits, a powdering tub, 2 old chests, a frying pan and a dripping pan, 5 pewter dishes, a basket, a comb and comb case, 2 doz trenchers and a basket, 2 pairs *barr ferris*, a box, 2 drinking glasses, a trunk, one pair of red taffeta curtains, an other pair of green satin curtains, a brass kettle, a pair of cob irons, 2 baskets with certain broken earthen dishes and some waste spices, $\frac{1}{2}$ lb. of white and blue starch, a vessel with two gallons of vinegar, 3 glass bottles, 2 stone jugs whereof one broken, a little iron pot and a great spit.'[64]

Later inventories show how this lack of possessions was a continuous feature of life in rural Ireland.

As rural Ireland settled into the modern pattern in the eighteenth century after the wars, pestilences and famines of the Tudor–Stuart period, new life styles were established to conform with the new political reality. Different tenurial arrange-ments were made and new systems of land holdings were established. The bulk of the rural population became tenants or labourers in a country where large estates dominated the landscape. What the standard of living was for the majority of rural dwellers in the eighteenth century is a matter of debate, but by the early nineteenth century poverty was the dominating factor in rural Ireland. The effect of that poverty was that many people lost what few possessions they had[65] and grinding poverty gave no encouragement to country people to even try to copy the furniture or ornaments of the mansions (pl. 27). It was only with post-famine improvements in the economic state of Ireland that many houses began to acquire luxury items or indeed manufactured goods of any kind. The history of furniture in rural Ireland offers little by way of high art, design or craftsmanship, though the exist-ence of carpenters of high technical competence is clearly seen in the work done in mansions like Adare Manor or in the practical crafts of the cartmaker and wheel-wright.

# 3 The Day's Work

The house in rural Ireland was more than just a place to eat and sleep in, it was also a workshop in which a wide variety of occupations were followed. The weavers' houses in the north of Ireland are the most obvious examples of this dual role of rural houses. In such houses all the implements for preparing wool were found side by side with ordinary furniture, and yet these houses were at one time common in many areas and indeed every house was a workshop of one kind or another. Most houses had all the tools necessary for converting the sheep's fleece into at least spun wool, and for converting the wheat from the field into ground meal. In an age before specialization most rural dwellers were capable of turning their hands to many crafts and the basic tools required for carpentry, harness-making, rope-making, stone-work, basket-making and churning were to be found in most houses (pls. 32–5).

The hearth was the workshop for the household cook. In modern times most meals were cooked on the open fire. The shortage of metal mentioned in the last chapter was not a serious problem from about 1700 when iron became plentiful and iron pots, pans and spits became common features in most houses. Two methods of suspending cooking vessels over the fire were employed in Irish traditional houses—the crane and the crook. The upright cranes were usually made of iron, though wooden ones were occasionally found. Cranes were fixed to the wall on one side of the fire so that the arm could be swung over the fire in any required position. By means of a hook sliding on the crane arm, vessels could be hung over the fire. One of these hooks was usually adjustable so that the vessel could be brought nearer or further from the fire. Handles for raising or lowering vessels were found on a few fire cranes. With a crane a number of vessels can be hung on it at the same time, and it can be swung out into the room to enable a person to remove boiling pots without stooping over the fire. The crook was a commoner and probably older device in Ireland. It was suspended above the hearth from a beam of wood which ran across the chimney at a safe distance over the fire. As with the fire crane the hooks used were usually adjustable and more than one pot could be hung over the fire at the same time (pls. 36–8).

With the exception of the kettle, almost all vessels used with cranes were provided with two small handles, and one or more pairs of pot-hooks. This was a necessary part of the cooking equipment as it meant they could be hung over the fire. The utensils included a number of cast-iron three-legged pots and these ranged in capacity from half a gallon to twenty gallons. The larger ones were used to boil

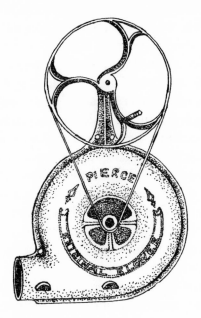

*Fig. 8. Wheel bellows or fire fan, Co. Wexford.*

food for pigs, for dyeing wool for home spinning and for boiling water for washing blankets and heavier clothes. The pot oven was primarily intended for baking but could also be used for roasting or boiling; griddles and bread stands or sticks were also used for baking bread. A frying pan, tongs, bellows, poker, hearth brush and trivet for griddles in some areas, completed the hearth furniture of the typical Irish house. The bellows were often of the wheeled variety and Pierce's of Wexford, who were Ireland's leading manufacturers of agricultural implements in the early nineteenth century, popularized a cast-iron wheel bellows which found its way to many thatched houses in Munster and parts of Leinster (fig. 8).

The tradition of cooking on the open hearth is well established in Ireland. Yet, as mentioned earlier, it is certain that before iron became cheap and plentiful outdoor cooking was just as common and boiling of food was done mainly in skins, wooden containers and occasionally in *fulachta fiadha*. *Fulachta fiadha* were ancient cooking sites where stones were heated and dropped into water in a wooden trough until the water boiled. In this way meat could be cooked or milk boiled[1] and food could also be cooked in a cowhide bag in the same way.[2] The alfresco tradition of cooking was strong in Ireland and of course meat and vegetables could also be cooked on spits without any containers. Spits were common in ancient Ireland and were widely used.[3]

The traditional house was also the dairy, and fresh milk was brought there and placed in earthenware pans, wooden stave-built keelers, or turned wooden bowls. Wooden skimmers were used to remove the cream after it had settled for buttermaking, and every house had a churn. The common type of Irish churn was a stoutly built stave vessel more or less conical in shape with a splayed neck into which the lid fitted. The cream was agitated by a wooden dash provided with a long handle which passed through a hole in the centre of the lid. The person churning stood beside the churn, grasped the handle with both hands and worked it up and down (pl. 40). The 'joggler', which was shaped like an inverted bowl with a hole in the top, sat on the lid and caught any liquid that may have splashed out. Curiously, the metal containers in which farmers still bring milk to creameries are similar in shape to the old dash-churns. The earlier type of Irish churn appears to have been a small vessel, round or square in plan, hollowed out of a single piece of wood, except for the bottom which was inserted. The lid, also cut from a single piece of wood, was provided with a sort of neck to accommodate the staff of the dash, and sometimes with a pair of handles as well. A churn was excavated from a rath in Co. Antrim and stray finds of containers, which may either have been churns or containers for butter, have been recorded from many areas in Ireland.[4] Dash-churns, even in the recent past, displayed a wide variety of styles, sizes and shapes in different areas in Ireland. The actual dash varied enormously from place to place as Evans has illustrated.[5] The task of churning was very laborious and many ingenious methods were devised to lighten the labour. Attaching the handle of the churn to a pole on a heavy spring meant that the principle of the pole lathe engine could be used in butter-making (pl. 39). Donkey and horse powered churns also became popular in the last century and some of these were in use up to the last decade (pl. 41). The actual churn used with all of these devices was still the old dash-churn, but this gave way on larger farms in the last century to beautifully manufactured barrel-churns.[6] These as the name implies consisted of a large barrel on a stand which was rotated on its axis by means of a crank handle (pl. 42); the milk inside was agitated by means of fixed flanges. The country coopers copied these manufactured articles so that many

*Fig. 9.* Top: *Dash-churn, Clonbern, Co. Galway.* Bottom: *Barrel-churn, Ennis, Co. Clare.*

D

crude examples are also found (fig 9). Tumble-churns were smaller barrel-churns which rotated on the other axis of the barrel and were sometimes known as end-over-end-churns. Finally a smaller type of cylindrical churn, in which the milk was agitated by a wooden frame with a crank handle, became popular in the present century. Today most milk is sent to the creameries and country butter is difficult to find, but it is still extremely popular and tastes completely different from that made in modern hygienic factories. After churning, country butter was usually

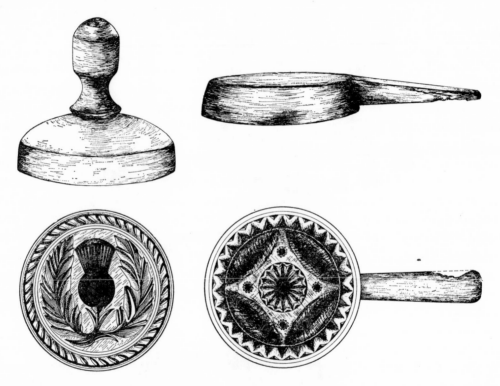

*Fig. 10. Butter prints of thistle and geometric design, Co. Donegal.*

taken out and washed. It was then often salted in large wooden bowls, being worked in the process with a wooden butter spade, the side of a small wooden bowl or with a mushroom-shaped butter worker. When finished the butter was given a decorative touch from the designs on the wooden stamps (fig. 10) and small balls of butter called 'patties' rolled between butter pats were often used for serving at the table. Butter has played an important part in the lives of people in rural Ireland at all periods, and in the eighteenth and early nineteenth centuries the butter market in Cork was one of the largest in the world at the time. Country farmers stored their butter until they had enough to take there. Its economic importance declined in the nineteenth century but has revived again in the present century.[7] Creameries organized on a co-operative basis are found in every county in Ireland and Irish butter is exported far and wide.

The tools required to convert grain after harvesting into edible foodstuff were also found in every house, however small. The most usual method of removing the grain from the straw in rural Ireland was by threshing with a flail (pls. 43 and 45), though a sixteenth-century account notes that the Irish did not thresh their oats but burned them from the straw.[8] Photographs from the early part of this century also show grain being removed by beating the sheaves on a stone (pl. 44). Both burning and lashing methods continued until this century and are proof of the strength of continuity of ancient techniques and practices. As with all ancient techniques many arguments are advanced to demonstrate the superiority of this procedure—burning dried the grain and lashing left straw which was ideal for thatching. The flail, however, was the universal threshing implement in Ireland as elsewhere in Europe until the introduction of the threshing machine in the nineteenth century. It consists of two sticks, a handstaff which is held in the hand and a beater which strikes the corn. The sticks are loosely tied together at their upper ends. The handstaff was usually made of ash and the beater of holly or hazel. The methods used for tying the two parts of the flail together differed from province to province and it is possible to identify the area of origin of a flail from the method of tying. In Ulster the tying was bound to the striker and either laced through a hole in the handstaff or, as in Connaught, attached to a groove near the end of the handstaff. In Munster the tying consisted of two interlocking loops, one attached to a groove near the end of the striker and the other similarly joined to the handstaff. In Leinster each stick was fitted with a loop at the end and a separate piece joined the two loops. In many flails the tying was arranged in such a way as to allow the beater or striker to rotate easily around the handstaff. The material used for the tying also varied. Thong, hide, goatskin, hay-rope and eel-skin were all popular. Flails were usually to be found hanging behind the door in traditional houses though they were usually used in pairs on sheaves of corn laid on the hard roadway outside. After threshing the husks were separated from the grain by winnowing. This operation was usually carried out on a windy day out of doors and the grain was tossed in the air from a winnowing tray made from a thin wood or a hazel rod bent into a circle and covered with a goat skin (pl. 46). The construction and appearance of this tray closely resembled the *bodhrán*, which is a popular percussion instrument. Wooden sieves made entirely of material found locally were also used,[9] and both sieves and trays were a common sight in traditional houses before being commercially produced. Winnowing machines began to appear from small factories or workshops in centres like Dungarvan, Co. Waterford, at the end of the last century. Though corn-grinding water mills, usually horizontal and of simple construction, were known in Ireland from the Celtic period,[10] the usual method of grinding was with hand querns. Mills with vertical wheels were introduced in medieval times yet two horizontal mills or gig mills were still in use in the Ballyhaunis area of Co. Mayo until 1906. The earliest hand-mills or querns used in Ireland from about 4000 BC onwards were probably the saddle querns in which a round stone rubber was rocked inside a hollow saddle-shaped lower stone. In rotary querns the upper stone revolves on the lower and the stone-ground meal is forced out at the sides and usually collected on a clean linen sheet. Rotary querns are mentioned by Virgil and were probably introduced into Ireland in Celtic times. Thousands of such stones were to be found in Ireland and itinerant craftsmen often called to dress the crushing surfaces of the stones, which became smooth from use and so became ineffective. Querns were also part of the equipment which made the kitchen the workshop in rural Ireland. These continued in use in remote parts of Ireland until the end of the nineteenth century and in Scotland until the mid nineteenth century.[11]

Self-sufficiency was the key-note of living through the centuries in rural Ireland. Even the smallest articles of everyday use could be made by countryfolk. Combs, which are now mass-produced and lost or discarded without thought, were laboriously made in many districts. An account from Tullokyne, Co. Galway, describes the process.

'They would boil the cow's horn first, and then when it became soft, they would flatten it out then while it was in that state, they would cut it up in the form of a comb. That was easily done. They used to have something like a crude knife and split it and allow it to harden. They had a small piece of handle. They used to scrub them with coarse salt. It used to give them a lovely colour, and a lovely shine. Twelve teeth they used to have in them.

'They used to mount them in silver in Galway. Some of them made them as a trade and sold them for 6d or 9d. A half sovereign would be got for a really ornamental one. I saw them when I was a child. It was commonly done around here. A *cóir* is what they were called.'[12]

Combs made in this manner were obviously valued possessions to be carefully looked after. Horn working could also produce spoons which were widely used, and decorative powder horns sometimes delicately carved were also made. Trumpet horns were made for giving signal calls for Mass on Sundays, and in the south-east horns were blown in the hills around the honeymoon house as a sign of local disapproval of a marriage. This usually happened when there was an excessive difference between the ages of the marriage partners. What a pity it is that those who follow the bridal party in motor cars with horns blaring could not be persuaded that in folk tradition this is a sign of disapproval!

The kitchen in the traditional house was witness to a wide variety of such rural crafts. The basket-maker's wares were widely used and the simple tools necessary for basket-making were found in every home. Baskets were usually made out of doors while the material was seasoned; rods were often kept in the kitchen corner. In some areas a wooden base on which baskets were built was found in many homes. Many country people were excellent thatchers and thatching needles, rakes, mallets and other tools were a common sight (pl. 51). Rope twisters were used for making ropes from a wide variety of local materials, and they were known in the northern counties as *thraw-hooks*. These were made in all kinds of shapes and materials[13] (pl. 52), and consisted basically of a hook at the end of a cranked handle; ropes were made by twisting straw, hay, rushes, bog-wood, horse hair, flax or indeed any suitable fibrous material. Ropes were important in a simple rural society and were used to secure thatch, to carry loads, to tie animals, to make mats, harness, seats for chairs and for innumerable other uses (pls. 53–4). Plate 55 shows a ball of rope, and its very size indicates the wide use made of such ropes. Bogdeal ropes, made from timber dug up from bogs, were very sturdy and Danaher has described this process.[14] Lighter lines for fishing were sometimes made from horsehair, and on the west coast an implement known as a *cairt* was used to twist several lines together to make a stronger line. This consisted of a frame containing a number of spindles each having a hook at its lower end, and the lines to be twisted together were attached to the hooks. A continuous loop of cord passed through a hole in one side of the frame and around each spindle in turn. By pulling the cord the spindles revolved and twisted the lines together. These were widely used on the west coast from Kerry to Mayo in former times.

Tools for many other small household crafts were to be found in country kitchens. Until recent years many country people had a last for repairing shoes or boots, and it was on this distinctive three-legged cast-iron piece that country boys hammered on their choice of pattern in hobnails to the soles of their boots. Leather working needles and sharp knives were also kept and most people knew how to treat thread with wax to make it waterproof and strong. For other items of dress the tools required for making and repairing were found everywhere. Hackles for carding wool were common, and big woollen spinning wheels were prized possessions in many houses. Tubs for thickening, dying and washing wool

were essential for the self-sufficient rural dweller. Iron pots and wooden tubs large
enough for washing clothes were kept, and traditional methods of cloth prepara-
tion continued for a long period. Even the pictorial evidence shows the antiquity
of many techniques in use till recent times (fig. 11 and pl. 59). Looms were not
found in every house and weaving was a specialized trade—although primitive
weaving was carried out in certain areas by every family until recently. One of the

*Fig. 11. Seventeenth-century sketch of girls washing clothes.*

gaps in our knowledge of the past, is that we know little about how much the
communities depended on specialist craftsmen in Gaelic Ireland. Because of the
widespread knowledge of many crafts it is possible that the specialist craftsmen
may only have emerged in recent times and that up to the year 1800 many rural
communities had no such separate group. The house, and especially the kitchen,
has always been more than a place to eat and sleep; it was always the workshop,
and indeed the place of entertainment, for past generations of countrymen and
women. The countryman's lore was handed down with a deep sense of respect

and carried with it the dignity of antiquity. Much of this lore was of a supernatural nature, yet much of it was practical. The great store of country cures has still to be published, though Logan has given a fascinating introduction to it.[15] A common complaint in rural Ireland was a wrist pain variously described as *trálach* or *tálach*. Weavers, farm workers and labourers suffered from this.[16] The greatest sufferers, however, were the road labourers of fifty years ago who sat with great heaps of stones at the side of the road and whose job was to laboriously break the stones with hammers. Country lore offered many cures for this pain, and to prevent it stone breakers were advised to fit furze handles to their hammers.

It was by the hearth in the traditional house that such lore was handed down and it was here also that many of the skills and crafts were practised. The diversity of the countryman's round of daily activities can be illustrated from a diary of John Joly. He recorded that in one day in 1847 he bought corduroy for trousers, thatched hay cocks, flew a kite, turned a spindle, mended a box barrow, went to the forge for nails, made a drum, played a drum and fiddle, turned wood and made flutes.[17]

# 4 Costume

Nothing impresses a tourist more than the sight of someone dressed in national costume. In a world in which the twin assaults of jeans from the west and the Mao-style uniforms from the East have reduced much of humanity to a drab uniformity, it is refreshing, and even startling, to see someone dressed in national costume. With few exceptions, European national costumes make use of bright, joyful colours. Primary colours are used to create intricate patterns in contrasting materials, and these beautiful garments clearly indicate that the wearer is a member of a distinctive ethnic group. This is essentially what a national costume is—an attempt to identify with either an ethnic group, a social class or a section of a community. The clothes are usually distinctive and of a type no longer worn except on festive occasions.

Many romantics have wished for an Irish national costume, but in spite of many attempts to establish certain items of dress as traditional, there is no generally accepted form of national dress. Irish nationalists at the end of the last century in common with their counterparts in western Europe were eager to establish their separateness in dress as well as in language, habits and customs. The erroneous idea of the kilt being traditionally Irish began and tartans became popular due to the activities of the Gaelic revival movements of the late nineteenth century.[1] For a time kilts became fashionable and many of the rebellion leaders of 1916 were seen wearing them. In 1908 Eamonn Ceannt wore a kilt when playing the uileann pipes for the Pope,[2] but this attempt to create a national costume failed. It is ironic that the knee breeches, tail coats and Caroline hats for men, and cloaks, red petticoats, shawls and aprons for women, which were popular at the time, were not considered as they lacked the distinctive Irishness which was so essential to those interested in the subject. The Irish poor were often caricatured in this garb.[3] Yet it is true that many national costumes are derived from attempts by labouring classes to imitate the fashion of the aristocracy, and as Paine has pointed out in a Welsh context, national costume often contains elements from many lands.[4] Peasant dress of the late nineteenth century has as much claim to be an Irish national costume as some of the more garish creations to be seen on occasion in the country. It is doubtful if a national costume can be created, as it is something which must evolve, and this certainly has not happened in Ireland. The everyday clothes of people in Ireland at the present time display few differences from the uniform garb of the Anglo-Saxon world. Any description of costume in Ireland is an account of traditional dress which under other circumstances might have become national costume.

It is difficult to describe costume in any country as it varies with class, age, sex, occupation and the evolution of style, fashion and materials. In Ireland the problems are increased by the paucity of visual evidence, and literary sources are both vague and brief. These problems have caused dress to be a neglected topic, but the few who have written about it have been thorough and accurate. Perhaps the first serious attempt to examine dress was made by Walker in the early nineteenth century. Describing his quest for sources he wrote:

'I visited the couch of the aged, and patiently listened to "the tale of other times"; I trimmed the midnight lamp over many a dry annalist, and pored with unremitting attention on many a musty manuscript; I explored the mouldering walls and "long sounding aisles" of cloistered fanes, for figures illustrative of my subject— nay, I even unbarred the gates of death and entered the tomb in quest of evidence.'[5]

In the fashion of the age the present writer has followed no such paths but has relied on the work of Walker, McClintock and other authors.

There is little archaeological evidence of costume in prehistoric Ireland. It is tempting to state that man's earliest clothes were made from the skins and hides of animals, but it is just as likely that they were made from platted grasses, hair, straw or indeed any other organic material. Many people displayed great skill in platting and weaving straw and wood in recent times and it seems probable that these skills were ancient in origin. Although there are few remains of textiles or fabrics of any kind from prehistoric Ireland, there is evidence that by the Bronze Age a sophisticated form of weaving had evolved. Bronze Age fabric made from unspun horsehair and found at Armoy, Co. Antrim, is woven in a herring-bone twill design, and weaving combs and spindle whorls that have been excavated indicate extensive knowledge of weaving in the Iron Age.[6]

The first real indication of the type of dress worn is to be found much later on. 'Earliest Irish dress' is the usual name given to this apparel, which is described in early Irish literature and is portrayed in illuminated manuscripts and sculptured stones. There is little to indicate when these forms of dress became popular, but whatever their origin two styles were popular in pre-Norman Ireland. It has been suggested that one form was indigenous while the other was introduced by the Celts.[7] Besides having different origins the two forms were worn by distinctive social groupings. The mantle and tunic were worn by the upper classes and the jacket and trews were worn by the young, the active and the lower orders.[8] The mantle was a large woollen sleeveless outer garment usually semi-circular or rectangular in shape and fastened with a brooch or pin either at the neck or on the shoulder. This could wrap around the body and could both cover the head and reach down to the ankles. The tunic was an inner garment resembling a shirt, often with wide hanging sleeves and dyed yellow; it reached to the knee when fastened with a *crious* or belt. Though the second form of dress is not mentioned in early Irish literature, it is represented on high crosses such as those at Monasterboice. The trews or trousers were generally tight fitting and varied in length between full and knee length; little is known about the jackets. Illustrations from the medieval period display a variety of shapes and sizes—some were short with a pleated skirt of about a foot long, while others were short, coming only to the waist. Some were collarless, while others had roll collars. In pre-Norman Ireland these two forms of dress were worn and it is interesting to speculate that the Celts may have introduced the mantle and tunic which replaced the jacket and trews of the older inhabitants of the island. It is assumed that women's dress in this period differed little from the male costume, and the mantle and tunic were certainly favoured by gentlewomen.

A wide variety of bright colours were worn and a person's position in society could be determined by the number of colours he was permitted to wear. Peasantry and soldiers were allowed only one colour, military officers and private gentlemen two, commanders of battalions three, self-sufficient farmers in clientship to a lord and keepers of houses of hospitality four, the principal nobility five, the bards and masters of the arts of poetry, law and learning six and kings and princes of the blood seven.[9] Red, purple and yellow were greatly favoured, and blue, green, brown, grey, black and golden are also recorded. Woad was a source of blue dye, and an extensive knowledge of vegetable and mineral dyes was a feature of life and tradition in rural Ireland until recent times.[10] Further decoration was added to these clothes by embroidery, trimmings, fringes and stripes. Wool was the most popular material, but linen and silk cloths were also woven.

Shoes, as some writer remarked, are probably as old as feet and were worn in pre-Norman Ireland at least by the more prosperous. At no period in Irish history could it be said that the Irish as a whole went barefoot and there is a vast amount of evidence to show that footwear was common. It has been suggested that there was more barefootedness in the country in the poverty-stricken nineteenth century than at any other time. Sufficient numbers of shoes have been found in datable contexts in Ireland to enable a typographical study to be made. Lucas has divided these survivals from archaeological sites into five clearly defined categories[11] (fig. 12), and these can be separated by the method of construction. All except the fifth type are made from a single piece of leather or rawhide. Tanning methods were well known in Ireland from earliest times, but in all periods tanned as well as untanned shoes were used in different areas and perhaps by different classes. The first three types of shoes illustrated are all from the early centuries of this era, and the most ornate of these became extinct in the early Christian period, perhaps around AD 700. The third type, a crude rawhide shoe, was also worn in the early Christian period and is still worn in the Aran Islands where such shoes are called 'pampooties' (pl. 59). The earliest evidence for the built-up shoe with a separate sole is in the sixteenth or seventeenth century. Shoes worn by the native Irish were invariably known as brogues, though no clear distinction between brogues and shoes can be drawn. Brogues were usually described as crude, and were always cheaper to buy. The crafts of making each were also separate, and nailed boots were introduced from America in the nineteenth century. Of all the aspects of traditional Irish dress, some of the shoes made in the early Christian period are the most beautiful in design and workmanship.

Hats and hoods of various types were also popular and the cloaks with hoods attached were distinctively Irish. The first description of Irish dress by a foreign writer is that given by Giraldus Cambrensis in the 1180s. His description has been translated as follows:

'For they wear but little woollen and nearly all they use is black that being the colour of the sheep in this country. Their clothes also are made after a barbarous fashion. Their custom is to wear small close-fitting hoods, hanging below the shoulders a cubits length, and generally made of particoloured strips sewn together. Under these they use woollen rugs instead of cloaks, with breeches and hose of one piece, or hose and breeches joined together, which are usually dyed of some colour.'[12]

With this unsatisfactory, contradictory but colourful account we leave early Irish dress.

The coming of Christianity caused little change in dress among the ordinary people. Clerics, however, adopted the manner of dress of their continental colleagues. There is little to indicate that either the Vikings or the Normans were to have any dramatic impact on habits of dress in rural Ireland. The Norman barons were constantly trying to prevent their followers from adopting the manners and customs

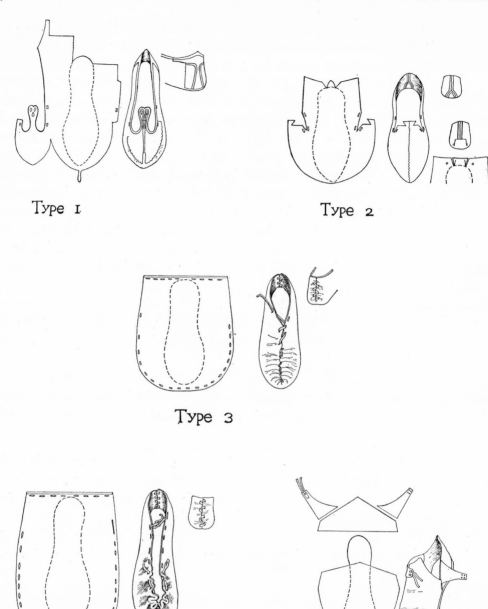

Type 1

Type 2

Type 3

Type 4

Type 5

Fig. 12. Irish shoe types. After Lucas.

of the older inhabitants. Just as full beards were identified with the older settlers
so also were certain forms of dress, and consequently both were suspect. Statutes

*Fig. 13. Sketch of medieval kings and workers.* Top: *Fowling.* Middle: *Ploughing.* Bottom:
*Digging and threshing with flails.*

prohibiting the wearing of Irish dress and Irish-style beards in Norman or Anglo-
Irish districts were still being enacted in the seventeenth century.[13] The frequency
with which such laws had to be re-introduced shows both the futility of such
measures and the tenacity of clothing habits and customs.

The traditional forms of dress were used throughout the medieval period by both natives and settlers alike, and an interesting medieval sketch shows a number of figures at work and play (fig. 13). The pair at the top are obviously kings or princes with crowns, wearing tunics, with the bottom section forming short pleated skirts. The third figure ploughing is wearing a short jacket with full sleeves, tunic, hood and shoes. The fourth figure, digging with a spade, is wearing a cape-like hood with three large buttons, pleated tunic and shoes. The pair at the bottom using flails on a sheaf of corn are dressed in what appear to be belted tunics. The tunic and mantle remained popular throughout this period, though the tunic was invariably fastened at the waist by a belt; jacket and trews also continued as popular items of dress. From the sixteenth century there are numerous descriptions of dress, and illustrations showing some detail appear for the first time (pl. 61). The new English who came to Ireland in Tudor times to begin the reconquest of Ireland not only became agents of change but also recorded their observations of the old inhabitants. William Good, who came as a missionary to Ireland in the 1560s, wrote:

'They generally go bare-headed save when they wear a head piece, having a long head of haire, with curled *gleebes*, which they highly value and take it hainously if one twitch or pull them. They wear linnen shifts, very large with sleeves down to their knees, which they generally dye with saffron. They have woollen jackets, but very short; plain breeches close to their thighs; and over these cast their mantles or shag-rugs—fringed with an agreeable mixture of colours, in which they wrap themselves up and sleep upon the bare ground. Such also do they women cast over the garment which comes down to their ankles, and the load their heads rather than adorn them, with several ells of fine linnen rolled up in wreaths, as they do their necks with necklaces and their arms with bracelets.[14]

The turbulent years of the Tudors were to witness the destruction of the Gaelic aristocracy. By the seventeenth century English law and influence began to spread once more outside the Pale. 'The civil assemblies at the assizes and sessions', wrote Sir John Davies, 'reclaimed the Irish from their wildness; caused them to cut their glibs and long hair, to convert their mantles into cloaks; and to conform themselves to the manner of England in all their behaviour and outward forms.'[15] Change was most notable in men's dress as traditional costume was gradually dropped in favour of contemporary English fashion.[16] This can be seen from some of the clothes preserved in the National Museum, and from the fully clothed body of a man who was recently found in a bog in Co. Sligo. He was wearing a wool felt hat, a tabby weave brown overcoat, jacket and breeches, a pair of woollen stockings, a pair of woven garters and a pair of shoes of untanned hide.[17] His costume—which dated from the seventeenth century—as a whole bore more resemblance to English costume of the period than to any Irish costume.

Men's costume in the eighteenth century continued to be modelled on the dress of the English aristocrats of the age and was copied by the poor in Ireland. By the nineteenth century a style of men's dress had evolved which was to become almost a national costume. This consisted of tightly fitting knee breeches, a 'swallow-tail' coat, a Caroline hat and brogues or hob-nailed boots. By the nineteenth century also, costume became adequately described and illustrated; the era of the tourist had arrived and even parliamentary commissions of inquiry were interested in costume. A composite picture of men's dress could be drawn from a variety of such descriptions and illustrations. Coats were almost universally made of frieze, but the colour varied. Blue was perhaps the most popular with light, dark, powder, azure and Windsor all mentioned as variants of this one colour. Blue mixed with white, brown, grey, black and damson is also recorded. The range of colours was large and friezes of colours such as white, grey brown, 'pepper and salt' and 'dark snuff' were described. Breeches were usually made of dark corduroy and sometimes of frieze. Waistcoats, which increased in fashion during the nineteenth century, were also made of corduroy, frieze or of cotton usually known as Manchester cotton. Buttons were usually made of brass. Woollen stockings are described as blue, white or brown and shirts are invariably white or blue. These costumes were the fashion, but with the appalling poverty in Ireland in the nineteenth century much of the population was dressed in rags.[18] Clothes, regardless of fashion, were worn for a long time and being frequently patched, people generally presented a tattered appearance. With patching, hard-wearing friezes could last a man a lifetime and when poverty prevented people buying new clothes it became essential to extend the usefulness of old clothes for as long as possible.

Women's dress was less affected by change in the modern period. Perhaps the best description in the early modern period is Luke Gernon's written in 1620:

'I proceed to theyr gowns. Lend me your imaginacon, and I will cutt it out as well as the tayler. They have straight bodyes, and longe wasts, but theyre bodyes come no closer but to the middle of the ribbe, the rest is supplyed with lacing, from the topp of their breasts, to the bottome of theyre plackett, the ordinary sort have only theyr smockes between, but the better sort have a silke scarfe about theyre neck, which they spread and pinne over theyre breasts. On the forepart of those bodyes they have a sett of broad silver buttons of goldsmiths worke sett round about. A sett of those buttons will be worth 40s. Some are worth £5. They have

hanging sleeves, very narrow, but no arming sleeves other than theyre smocke
sleeves, or a wastcoate of stripped stuffe, onely they have a wrestband of the same
cloth, and a lyst of the same to ioyne it to their winge, but no thing on the hinder
part of the arme least they should weare out theyr elbowes. The better sort have
sleeves of satten. The skyrt is a piece of rare artifice. At every bredth of three
fingers they sew it quite through with a welte, so that it seemeth so many lystes
putt together. That they do for strength, they girde theyr gowne with a silke
girdle, the tassell whereof must hang down poynt blanke before the fringe of
theyr peticotes . . . They beginne to weare knitt stockins coloured, but they have
not disdayned to weare stockins of raw whyte frise, and broges. They weare
theyr mantles also as well within doors as without. Theyr mantles are commonly
of a browne blew colour with fringe alike, but those that love to be gallant were
them of greene, redd, yellow, and other light colours, with fringes diversified. An
ordinary mantle is worth £4, those in the country which cannot go to the price
weare whyte sheets mantlewise. I would not have you suppose that all the Irish are
thus strangely attyred as I have described. The old women are loath to be shifted
out of theyr auncient habitts, but the younger sort, especially in gentlemen's
houses, are brought up to resemble the English, so that it is to be hoped, that
the next age will weare out these disguyses.'[19]

Even in the nineteenth century the tight-laced bodice and the wide skirt, sometimes in one piece, were common. The tight-fitting jacket which became popular
in the late nineteenth century probably evolved from the bodice. Descriptions of
women's clothes in the last century can also be generalized, though this must be
done with caution as one writer has remarked that 'the inhabitants of one barony
are easily distinguishable by their peculiar dress from another'.[20] Women's dress
in the last century showed greater continuity with ancient Ireland than men's.
The hooded cloak, the garment evolved from the great mantle of antiquity, was
universally popular and was made of many different colours—black, blue, grey,
red and scarlet. It is now only worn as a black cloak where it survives in west
Cork. Originally cloaks were made of coarse frieze, but gradually finer fabrics
became more popular and broadcloth and pilotcloth were used.[21] Married women
usually wore some form of covering on their heads. Small linen or lace caps,
muslin caps, high cauled mop caps and handerchiefs of various colours were
worn (pls. 62 and 64). Single women generally went bareheaded and shoes when
worn were usually of the brogue type. In some districts footless stockings were
worn and during the century cotton stockings became fashionable for the more
affluent (pl. 63). Frieze was as popular with women as with men. Druggets and

27. *Evicted family and furniture c. 1890* (N.L.I. Imp. 1506).

28. *Two breadsticks, Co. Clare and Co. Galway.*

29. *Baking stone, Toneyloman, Co. Fermanagh* (N.M.I. EF105).

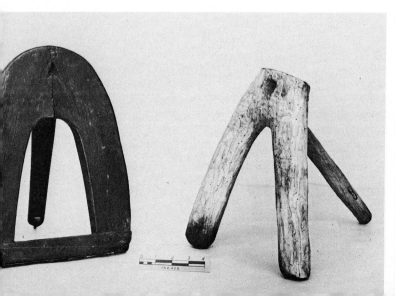

*30. Two hardening fenders (N.M.I. CF1).*

*31. Three breadsticks or stands, Ballymagaraghy, Co. Donegal, Meenacam, Co. Donegal, and Toneyduff, Co. Cavan (N.M.I. GF95).*

32. *Carding wool, Carrick, Co. Donegal*
(B.F. TY102/48).

33. *Weaving Aran crios (N.M.I. CF318).*

34. Bottom left: *McKeown's weaving industry, Leenane, Co. Galway*
(N.L.I. 6770WL).

35. Below: *Irish spinning wheel*
(N.L.I. 2565WL).

*36. Fireplace, Co. Galway* (B.F. TY*18*/*48*).

*37. Conagher's farm, Co. Antrim* (N.L.I. *6721*).

*38. Baking on an open fire*
(B.F. TY*11*/*48*).

39. *Spring churn at Clarke's farm, Cortial, Co. Louth (N.M.I. DF1953).*

40. *Dash-churn, Co. Kerry (N.M.I. EF181).*

42. *Tumble-churn, Ballintober, Co. Roscommon; cylindrical churn, Coonagh, Co. Limerick; dash-churn, Athlone, Co. Roscommon.*

41. *M. Halpin's donkey-powered dash-churn, Ardagh, Co. Longford (N.M.I. DF3196).*

*43. Man using flail, Tory Island (N.M.I. SF629).*

*45. Three flails (N.M.I. CF10).*

*44. Threshing corn by beating on stones, Aran Islands (N.M.I. CF333).*

*46. Winnowing corn with tray, Aran Islands (N.M.I. CF331).*

47. *Basket-making at Carna show, Co. Galway* (B.F. TY*190*).

48. *Wooden sieve, Brownsgrove, Tuam, Co. Galway* (N.M.I. DF*560*).

49. *Making willow baskets, Co. Donegal* (B.F. TY*62*).

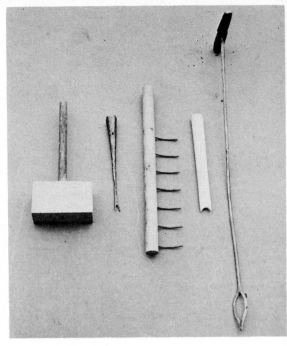

50. Baskets for different uses: hay basket, Co. Roscommon; skib, Co. Galway; calf basket, Co. Clare; birdeog, Co. Kerry; turf basket, Co. Sligo; skib, Co. Longford.

51. Thatchers' tools: mallet, Co. Longford; fork, Co. Meath; rake, Co. Dublin; stick Co. Wexford; needle, Co. Westmeath.

52. Suggan twisters (N.M.I. CF348).

53. *Straw-rope granary filled and ready for covering, Ahern's, Budderameen, Ballineen, Co. Cork (N.M.I. DF751).*

54. *Straw-rope granary completed (N.M.I. DF762).*

55. *Rope-making, Co. Donegal (B.F. TY61).*

56. *Irish costume, late nineteenth century* (N.L.I. *3136WL*).

57. *Hooded cloak, Kinsale, Co. Cork* (B.F. TY*143*).

58. *'Wash day', Keel, Achill, Co. Mayo* (B.F. TY*99/48*). *Compare with fig.* 11.

59. Above left: *Making a pampootie, Aran Islands, Co. Galway.*

60. Above right: *Woman's costume, Aran Islands. Plaid headscarf or shawl, grey tweed jacket with collar and cuffs of black velvet, navy-blue-grey apron, red woollen petticoat or skirt and pampooties. Modelled by Mrs Annie Adams* (N.M.I. EF304).

61. Left: *Six engravings of Irish costume from Speed's map of Ireland, sixteenth century.*

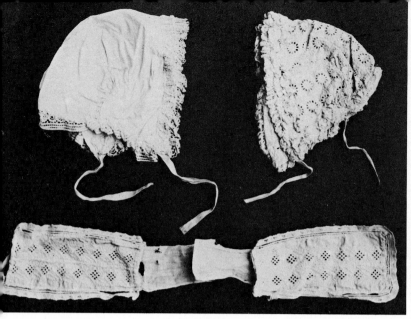

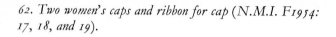

62. *Two women's caps and ribbon for cap* (N.M.I. F1954: 17, 18, and 19).

63. *Pair of soleless stockings, Ballina, Co. Mayo* (N.M.I. F1958: 13,

64. *Woman wearing cap* (N.L.I. 3159WL).

65. *Red petticoat.*

66. *Knitted shoulder shawl, Inishere, Aran Islands, Co. Galway* (N.M.I. F1957: 96).

67. *Skirt raised while churning to reveal drugget petticoat* (N.L.I. C9465).

68. *Best shawls on display going to confirmation, Carraroe, Co. Galway* (B.F. TY*255*).

69. *Children's costume. Notice boy in petticoat. Bartley Flaherty, Innishmaan, Aran Islands, Co. Galway* (B.F. TY*162*).

70. *Petticoat with crios worn as shawl*
*(N.M.I. CF509).*

71. *Co. Galway farmer and weaver*
*c. 1910. John O'Neill, Knocknagur,*
*Co. Galway.*

72. *Group of Aran Islanders.*

73. *Aran man and child* (B.F. TY71).

flannels were also popular while cotton came into common use in the last century. Gowns of cotton or linen were often worn over skirts of frieze or drugget and when working these were generally turned up and fitted into the waist band (pl. 67). The garment often called a red petticoat could be described as a skirt and was expected to be seen (pl. 65). Barrow, describing women in the Headfort area of Co. Galway, wrote:

'The females in this part of the country as well as in Connemara, wear short red jackets and petticoats, the former reaching a little below the waist; or a gown is sometimes superadded, generally tucked up, as if purposely to show the bright red undergarment.'[22]

Indeed these were sometimes even worn as shawls over the head. Neck scarves were popular as were small shoulder shawls, which were usually worn over a blouse, the end being tucked inside the waist band of the skirt (pl. 66). Larger shawls also became popular in the last century and these replaced hooded cloaks as the normal outer garment in many areas. Plaid shawls in a variety of colours and patterns became popular in many areas (pls. 68 and 70). These have again declined in popularity and indeed are now only seen on Irish itinerant women in many areas.

As in most countries children's clothes were scaled down copies of adult garb. One exception to this was that small boys commonly wore dresses until the age of seven, and little boys and girls were indistinguishable except for the way in which their hair was cut (pl. 69). The explanation usually offered for this was that the fairy who sometimes took infant boys away to the land of youth would mistake the small boy with the dress for a girl and so would take no further interest. The custom of dressing boys in girl's clothing was not confined to Ireland but is also found in other European countries.

The general style of dress changed in the present century (pl. 71). Brogue makers and weavers of homespun wool disappeared as they lost their popularity and were unable to retain their ability to compete with mass-manufactured articles. Fashion designers have discovered the beauty of the hooded-cloak, but their influence has had little effect in popularizing it again. Wooden-soled boots, though no longer made, are imported to meet a small demand in Counties Cavan, Leitrim and Monaghan. Some men still favour coarse tweed suits, but these bear little resemblance to the frieze trousers and jackets of seventy years ago. Indeed, dress in Ireland has lost much of its traditional appearance and with notable exceptions has become indistinguishable from that worn generally in the western world; this has happened in materials as well as design, as nylon and man-made fibres have replaced traditional materials. This is just a generalized account of costume

E

and it omits much that is colourful, beautiful and artistic in Irish costume. In the early heroic literature we are told of Irish embroidery, and Emer's 'gift of embroidery and needlework' is listed as one of her great talents in the Cuchulainn tales, but unfortunately no example of the work of that period survives. In a later period, however, lace-making, crochet-work, ornate knitting and sophisticated silk-weaving were carried on and many examples of this work show both the craft and the artistic skill of their makers.[23] We know little of the skills of the earlier period, though Lucas has shown how fulling and napping methods of cloth finishing in Ireland continued in an unbroken tradition from pre-Norman to modern times.[24] Fulling is a process which gives cloth greater density and a softer finish, and napping is a process by which a nap or pile was raised on frieze or flannel after weaving. Fulling is carried on wherever cloth is woven, but napping gave Irish clothes their peculiar shaggy appearance which is so often described in the early accounts of Irish dress. Though more difficult to demonstrate it is probable that the skill displayed in spinning and weaving is also of great antiquity.[25]

As we shall see in a later chapter dressing up in unusual costumes forms part of the traditional celebrations on holidays and special occasions in Ireland. There was also ritual concerning the manufacture and use of ordinary clothes. Spinning, fulling and even knitting were traditionally processes carried out by groups of neighbours and such meetings became occasions of enjoyment and gaiety. There is a continuous history of such work sessions from the eighteenth century till recent times[26] and they often ended with a dance, a special meal and singing or storytelling. There were also unwritten rules about clothes. Best clothes were usually described as Sunday clothes and were always worn to Mass. Indeed in many areas it was considered unlucky to wear a new garment until it had first been worn to Mass. Summer clothes were usually worn from 1st May to 1st November. The change from winter to summer clothes for many people was very small and might have involved the shedding of one undergarment. Boys, who during the winter wore boots, might for these months go barefooted. Finally, of the many traditions concerning clothes, the fear of wearing second-hand clothes could be mentioned. This is probably a legacy of the days when terrible diseases were endemic in Ireland and people were afraid to wear second-hand clothes because of the risk of contagion.[27] The costume of people in parts of the west is an archaic survival which until recently resisted all influences of change. Here, the heavy homespun trousers are still worn along with pampooties or raw-hide shoes of very primitive construction; these are often worn with heavy jerseys which have achieved widespread popularity. Donegal and Aran jerseys were originally knitted by men, though now only women do this job. Knitted from undyed natural wool, and using as many as a dozen different stitches, jerseys with distinctive patterns were made—they are now usually knitted in white, black and navy. The variety of stitches on these jumpers enabled families to identify victims of drowning tragedies by the different patterns.[28] Over the top was worn a double-breasted jacket with braided edges, while in some areas a lightweight *bainín* or white woollen jacket was worn (pls. 72–3). In general no heavy jacket or overcoat was used as people preferred the sleeveless waistcoat as an outer garment. In these areas also heavy woollen shirts were often worn, although the popularity of this form of dress is now decreasing. Younger people do not wear these clothes—materials for making them are difficult to obtain and even the knowledge of how to make them is now almost lost.

Fashion in rural Ireland throughout the centuries was the concern of the wealthy members of the community. From the sixteenth century on such people were influenced by English and continental fashions. Yet the majority of country people were primarily interested in clothes which were warm and hard-wearing. Inevitably the fashions of the aristocracy had some effect, as had the new materials. In the more affluent twentieth century, fashion is no longer an exclusive symbol of aristocracy but is rather the norm for the great mass of the population. Though it is difficult to say what dictates change in fashion it is now certain that Ireland is open to all the factors which are usually described as being responsible for such change. People who now follow fashion are affected by the influence of designers and manufacturers, of individuals and public opinion, of foreign innovators and the textile industry in general. Multi-national department stores provide fashion for all strata of society. This has not always given us clothes which are either functional or pleasing, and it still remains possible for some designer to again popularize some of our traditional garments.

# 5 Food

If food is taken as the key element in Irish history, then the past falls into two great eras. The first, which stretches from Neolithic times to the seventeenth century, was a time when people relied on corn and milk as their principal foods. The second period followed the introduction of the potato, when this plant gradually began to replace corn and to a lesser extent milk as the staple diet of the majority of the people. As with so many aspects of life and tradition a third era may now be dawning as the potato declines in popularity. After its long period of calamitous supremacy Irish people, like their counterparts in western Europe, are turning to a varied diet of which corn, meat, potatoes, rice, fish and fowl are the staple items.

In Mesolithic times people were mainly fishermen and foodgatherers and little is known about their food. From Neolithic times cattle began to play a major role in Irish society and provided key elements in the diet of the people. The vast quantities of cattle bones, excavated from archaeological sites, prove the importance of cattle.[1] From the records of the early historic period a picture can be constructed of how cattle were used. Contrary to what might be expected, cattle were not reared primarily for beef. Cows made up the vast proportion of the cattle population, and bulls were reared only in small numbers for breeding and draft purposes. Beef was eaten, but as in the medieval period it seems likely that cattle were kept primarily for their milk.[2]

In this first era, milk was not only consumed as a drink while fresh, but was also used in a wide variety of ways. Many milk products were made and butter, cheese, curds and white meats were popular. A seventeenth-century commentator wrote of the Irish as 'generally being the greatest lovers of milk I ever saw, which they eat and drink about twenty several sorts of ways and what is strangest, love it best when sourest'.[3] In the medieval poem the *Vision of Mac Conglinne* many milk products are mentioned, and from this and other early Irish texts the various names used to describe milk products can be learned.[4] Cheeses were of the soft and pressed variety, but our knowledge of these is in some ways speculative as cheese-making died out in the eighteenth century; there is no continuous tradition of cheese-making in rural Ireland and it still has to regain its popularity in the diet of Irish country folk. In contrast with cheese, butter has retained its popularity and has always been eaten in enormous quantities in Ireland. In medieval times it was sometimes flavoured with garlic or onions, and butter buried in bogs is still occasionally found. Such butter developed a distinctive taste which presumably was enjoyed by those accustomed to eating it. Butter buried in bogs which afforded ideal storage conditions was also safe from plunderers,[5] and it may be for this reason that the practice began. From earliest times also, food was stored in souterrains or caves both for hygiene and safety.[6] Such caves bear no resemblance to the thermally insulated icehouses built for storing food by landlords in nineteenth-century Ireland.

One of the finest early records of food in Ireland is the twelfth-century poem the *Vision of Mac Conglinne* mentioned earlier. In the poem there are long lists of various foods with details of their preparations. Milk and milk products are mentioned most frequently and the other foods noted are those which were usually found in a simple rural society. The products of contempory farming are also listed.

Wheat, oats and barley are the only cereals mentioned; leeks, onions and carrots are the only vegetables; and apple and nut trees are the only fruit trees.[7] Honey, of course, was of great importance as the sweetening agent for many foods. In this first gastronomic era corn was the second staple element in the diet of the people. It was grown in Ireland from Neolithic times when characteristic saddle querns were used for grinding it. A Bronze Age pottery vessel, of the type known as a 'Food Vessel', excavated at Fourknocks bears the impression of a wheat seed on its outer surface, and so too does an example from Co. Wexford. Simple water mills, known as horizontal mills, were in use in Ireland as early as the seventh century, and in the medieval period similar water mills and hand querns were used for grinding corn.[8] Further evidence of the extensive use of corn is to be found in the references in early Irish literature to primitive corn-drying kilns, which were known in remote areas until relatively modern times.[9]

Oats, barley, wheat and rye were the types of corn used, and Lucas has argued that their economic importance in medieval Ireland was in that order;[10] they were eaten mainly as bread and porridge. Oaten bread was the most common type made, while barley bread was regarded as suitable for monks and others who wished to mortify themselves, and wheaten bread was regarded as a luxury. Porridge was as popular in medieval times as it is today in rural Ireland, despite the attractions of modern cereal breakfasts. Traditionally in Ireland porridge was not exclusively a breakfast food but was eaten in large quantities at midday, in the evening and also at supper before retiring to bed. Porridge was made from oats, wheat or barley, mixed with water, new milk, buttermilk or sour milk. It could be eaten hot or cold—as Danaher has observed—and either cooked or uncooked, fresh or fermented, very thick or in liquid form, flavoured with salt, sugar, butter, honey or herbs.[11] Though flails for threshing were well known in medieval Ireland, Derricke recorded that the Irish did not thresh their oats but burned them from the straw and afterwards made them into cakes.[12] After being ground into meal, corn was often sifted in a sieve to obtain finer flour for bread-making. Wooden kneading troughs called lossets were used in medieval Ireland and are still in use in the midland counties, but built-up baking ovens which had probably been introduced by the monastic orders were confined to the towns and villages in the east and south. When baking without an oven, bread was placed either on the growing coals or on a large cabbage leaf, or even on a flagstone in front of the fire. Here, the stone was heated by placing hot coals from the fire on it and then after they were removed the bread was placed on the hot stone. This operation was repeated on different parts of the flagstone until the bread was baked. Oaten bread was usually baked on edge in front of the fire, and the oaten cakes were supported in this position by a simple stand often crudely fashioned from a piece of triple-forked wood (pl. 28). In some areas beautifully carved stone stands have been found (pl. 29), and in the north of the country wrought-iron stands or specially designed fenders made by blacksmiths were popular (pl. 30). Stands for a single cake, known as breadsticks, consisted of an arched back against which the cake rested, and a small shelf at the bottom on which the cake stood. By means of a stay hinged at the top of the arch the stand could be propped in an almost vertical position on the hearth (pl. 34). The fenders—known as 'harnen' fenders, and presumably being a corruption of hardening fenders—were made to hold up four cakes and the two halves could be opened out to partly enclose the fire. Both breadsticks and fenders are fine examples of the folk art of the blacksmith's craft. In modern times, on the open hearth of the typical Irish house, bread was baked either in a pot oven called a 'bastable' or on a griddle. The pot oven was a cast iron pot with a flat bottom and tight-fitting lid, while the griddle was usually a circular flat iron with either one or two lugs or ears. Both the griddle and the pot oven could be either hung over the fire or rested on a trivet over the hot embers. If hung over the fire the pot oven was suspended by an ordinary pair of pot-hooks, but to hang the griddle a special set of hooks was sometimes used. When the pot oven was in use live embers were heaped on the lid so that the top of the cake was baked evenly with the bottom. If it was necessary to inspect the progress of baking it was possible to lift off the lid with a pair of tongs without disturbing the embers.

In Ireland the pig was kept exclusively as a domestic animal for its meat, while in parts of Scotland pig meat was never eaten. This particular taboo has been attributed to the Pictish origins of the people in the eastern and central Highlands, as the Gaelic and Norse settlers in Scotland had no such aversion to pork. Pig bones have been found at a Neolithic site at Sutton, Co. Dublin. Besides domestic pigs, wild swine were also hunted and both domestic and wild animals fed extensively on oakmast. Bacon, pork and different types of sausage were eaten and in Mac Conglinne's poem of the twelfth century there are numerous references to different types of meat from pigs. In one part of the poem Mac Conglinne describes a fort of his dreams:

> The fort we reached was beautiful,
> With works of custards thick,
> Beyond the loch,
> New butter was the bridge in front,
> The rubble dyke was wheaten white,
> Bacon the palisade.[13]

Mutton and beef were also eaten, but sheep were kept primarily for their wool and cows were valued most highly for their milk yield. Fishing was popular in medieval Ireland and many ancient fishing weirs have been recorded. Ireland exported large quantities of pilchards, hake, cod, herring and salmon to England and the Continent in the medieval period, although mackerel in great shoals only made its appearance in Irish coastal waters in the second half of the last century.[14] On an island such as Ireland with rivers, lakes and streams, fish from both sea or fresh water were usually available. All the wild fruits were eaten including the sloe, cherry, raspberry, strawberry, rowan, crabapple, elderberry, whortleberry, cranberry and especially the blackberry.

The most popular drinks in ancient and medieval Ireland were milk and whey. Ale has also been drunk throughout the ages, and wines were imported by the privileged few from Roman times. Distillation of whiskey probably began in the medieval period, and it is referred to in the annals for the first time in the year 1405.[15] While brewing no longer continues as a country craft, distillation still flourishes despite the sanctions of Church and State.[16]

Irish food, with milk and corn forming the staple diet, remained relatively unchanged until the introduction of the potato. It reached Europe in 1588 and tradition as well as some historical evidence links the name of Sir Walter Raleigh with its introduction to Ireland.[17] An academic debate among historians is currently continuing as to when the potato gained its dominant position in rural diet and Salaman, the pioneer in the study of the potato in Irish history, has claimed that potatoes were the ordinary food of the people as early as 1630.[18] Some argue that the rapid rise in population which began in the eighteenth century was due to the potato. Others maintain that the potato only gained universal popularity towards the end of the eighteenth century when population pressure forced people to abandon traditional methods of food production to support large numbers.[19] This argument revolves around the fact that a field planted with potatoes can sustain twice as many people as one planted with wheat. Whichever date is correct the potato gradually replaced all other foods as the staple article of diet. Eating habits changed, and some foods such as cheese and ale which had been used extensively for centuries were forgotten as Young found when he toured Ireland at the end of the eighteenth century.[20] Change in diet, which is usually one of the most difficult changes to achieve in society, had taken place and it seems certain that this could only have been brought about by the harshest economic necessity. In the seventeenth century war and revolt were the cause of many upheavals as plantations and land settlements led to changes in the ownership of land. The eighteenth century, though there were no wars, saw famine on the land, and as the population began to increase, holdings grew smaller and people moved to marginal land. Many produced only the bare essentials for survival and by the early nineteenth century a subsistence economy was well established. The potato was the thread on which people's hope for survival depended, and unlike grain which can be stored from year to year the potato only lasted for one year. In many districts, particularly in the south and west, people were not able to produce enough potatoes to last a full year and the summer months, between the exhaustion of the old year's supply and the harvesting of the new crop, became known as 'The Hungry Months'.[21] Famine and disease were commonplace and people suffered appalling deprivations.[22]

By 1845 the transition from grain to potatoes was complete, and on the eve of the Great Famine the country reached its point of greatest dependence on the calamitous tuber. Consumption was high, and on an average adults consumed ten pounds of potatoes per day when these were available.[23] It is estimated that at that time the country produced fifteen million tons of potatoes every year of which 47 per cent, or seven million tons, was used for human consumption. Of the remainder, 33 per cent was used as animal food, 13 per cent was needed for seed, 5 per cent was wasted and 2 per cent went in exports. A contributor to the Irish *Farmers' Journal* in 1846 estimated that over five million of the population of eight million depended entirely on potatoes,[24] although it must be stated that in parts of Ireland people never became completely dependent upon the potato. In these areas oatmeal continued to be the mainstay in the diet of the people and this was particularly true in parts of Ulster. The use of oatmeal and other grain produce had a social as well as a regional distribution and moving up the social scale a mixed diet of potatoes, milk, oatmeal and wheaten bread could be found among the farmers. Meat was a luxury enjoyed by few in Ireland on the eve of the Great Famine, and not many vegetables were grown. Cabbage achieved the immense popularity it still continues to enjoy in rural Ireland during the Great Famine, when it was sown as a safe crop instead of potatoes.

As with milk and milk products in an earlier age, a wide variety of preparations were used to vary the monotony of the potato diet. Potatoes were usually boiled, but they could also be roasted in the hot ashes of the fire. When boiled, mashed potatoes were mixed with cabbage, kale, onions, leeks and milk to make a dish known as colcannon, and a somewhat similar dish without green vegetables was known in the northern counties as champ. Potato cakes were made and were known by a wide variety of names in different areas. Bread or pancakes made from potatoes and flour could be cooked either on a griddle or in a pan and were known in many counties, particularly in the west, as 'boxty'. It would be impossible to list the full variety of ways in which potatoes were eaten as they were combined with every available food both to give variety and to supplement meagre supplies.

The potato solved Ireland's food problems for a long period but was an un-reliable crop as the Great Famine was to prove when potato blight ruined the crop in successive years. Even before the Great Famine the potato was often damaged by unfavourable weather conditions, and people were accustomed to seeking alternative food supplies. In coastal regions all the resources of the sea were used. A report of famine on the island of Arranmore, Co. Donegal, in 1836 said 'many families are living on cockles, periwinkles and other shellfish and some upon seaweed'.[25] Other reports tell of people risking life and limb to get sea birds or their eggs from cliffs[26] and descriptions of a coast crowded with people seeking whatever edibles they could find were quite common. In other areas a wide variety of wild plants were eaten, and Lucas has written that nettles and charlock were used extensively both as need foods and as regular articles of diet.[27] A feast provided in Tobermoney for men who helped to build a one-day sod house was composed of '*prushag milis*, and the soft tops of nettles boiled together from which the water was pressed, and butter added in plenty, was champed together'. This meal was eaten with wooden spoons and to finish the meal 'a good fire harned scon', washed down with plenty of milk, was added.[27a] Plants, nuts and seed, which in the pre-potato era had formed part of the regular diet of the people, were used again. The bleeding of cattle to obtain the blood as food was a common practice in Ireland, and it was often used in the war-years of the sixteenth century.[28] In many areas the husks of corn were collected by the poor for food, and when mixed with a little oatmeal and water this made a nourishing drink known as 'sowens'. Starvation in Ireland, as it does wherever it occurs, drove people to eat what they could, how they could and whenever they could, and even grass was eaten with disastrous results. In no other western European country is starvation caused by crop failure so fresh in the folk memory, and many older people are very much aware of the terror of famine. This is hardly surprising as the last famine in Ireland occurred as recently as the 1890s when parts of Kerry were badly affected.[29]

To describe Irish food as falling into two main periods is obviously a serious over-simplification as it does not take into account many aspects of food which are very important. Male and female, young and old, noble and peasant rarely have similar eating habits, and factors such as religion, work, economics and environment all influence diet. Even though people are certainly conservative in diet, it rarely remains static, and like other aspects of society it is constantly changing and developing.[30]

The connection between food and religion has always been strong in Ireland, and food was regarded as being God's gift and had to be treated as such. Grace before and after meals was an acknowledgment of this fact, and the custom of never refusing food to wandering beggars was regarded as a duty to God who provided all food.[31] This reliance on God's bounty was also acknowledged in other ways such as, when baking, a cross was always made on top of the cake and not to do so was, and indeed still is, regarded as unlucky.[32] Throughout Europe during medieval times people travelled with holy pictures around the fields to invoke blessings on the growing crops,[33] and in parts of Ireland it is still the custom to place medals of saints in the four corners of a field for similar purposes. Occasionally such medals may have been placed to ward off evil rather than to invoke God's blessing and in such cases this could be evidence of an even older tradition. Horseflesh, which early churchmen regarded as being associated with pagan rites, is still not eaten in Ireland.[34] Just as God had to be thanked for his gifts, it was also believed that famine was due to the will of God, and it was for this reason that Irish people accepted crop failure and starvation so placidly. Indeed even major epidemics were regarded as punishment by God for wrongdoing, and though such attitudes have now changed it is necessary to understand them if we are to catch a glimpse of the past.[35] In Ireland until recently, religious practice prevented consumption of meat by the majority of the population on Fridays, quarter days and during the season of Lent. At an early period Wednesdays were also days of abstinence from meat, and older country people still continue this practice.

Throughout the centuries fasting and abstaining from meat, eggs, butter and milk have been a regular feature of the lives of the people, and total abstinence from food for three days is still observed by pilgrims visiting the holy island of Loch Derg in Donegal.[36]

As in other countries different classes in Ireland had different food. 'Bakers' bread', as white loaves are called in parts of Ireland, were regarded as a luxury as they could only be purchased by the more affluent.[37] In parts of Tipperary the white loaf was known as 'priests' bread' as it was only purchased when the priest was about to visit a house to say Mass.[38] The majority of country people could only afford to bake their own brown bread. The tradition of only the upper class eating bakers' bread goes back to the seventeenth century.[39] It was not only in varieties of breads that class differences in diet were reflected. In the early nineteenth century Carleton described the food eaten in the house of wealthy farmers on special occasions as being geese and fowl of all kinds, shoulders of mutton, potatoes, carrots, parsnips and cabbage as well as an immense pudding boiled in a clean sheet.[40] This was at a time when the country's dependence upon the potato was at its highest, and it is hardly surprising that different eating habits were reflected in the appearance of different classes. In a poem in which he reflected upon his life, a wandering labourer said he was tired of sitting by the wall at the hiring fair waiting for big fat farmers to come and employ him.[41] The poet's reflections were supported by the evidence of one labourer in Co. Cork who said: 'The mean devils [the strong farmers], they would give you spuds [i.e. potatoes] and some milk and put you to do the hardest work and eat plenty of meat themselves and do the lightest.'[42]

Different foods were regarded as suitable for different types of work. A cake, as big as the wheel of an ass-cart and made with curds, butter and eggs, was prepared specially for groups of men cutting turf in the Killarney district.[43] Communal eating on occasions such as turf-cutting, threshing and harvesting when groups joined together often gave these meals a festive air. Nor was communal work confined to men, as women for example often gathered together for sessions spinning wool. Traditionally, when meat was carved, certain portions were reserved for specific people and the tradition of giving the head of a slaughtered beast to the blacksmith is a survival of an old custom.[44] Wayward boys were often threatened that they would get the 'bundun' or tail of a chicken if their behaviour did not improve and for small children a mixture of potatoes or bread and hot milk known as 'pandy' was often made.[45] Gingerbread and saffron cake were also made as a treat for children in Carlow.[46]

At weddings, feasts and festivals, when in general everything was presented on a large scale, special dishes were prepared. Christmas in the popular mind is now the holiday most closely associated with feasting, and the turkey, which came to Europe at the same time as the potato, is now the most important item in the Christmas dinner. Though turkeys were known in Ireland since the seventeenth century they only became associated with the Christmas dinner in the present century, and this development was probably caused by the writing of English Victorian novelists. The traditional Christmas dish before the turkey was beef, either roasted or boiled, and spiced beef is still popular in some areas at Christmas.[47] For the affluent, fowl were always popular and a goose or a chicken was regarded as a suitable Christmas delicacy. Puddings of various kinds have always been popular at Christmas and continue to be so. The nature of the Christmas food depended on the prosperity or otherwise of the family and on the customary dishes in the region; rye bread was always a traditional Christmas treat in Connemara.[48] Christmas Day was the main day of celebration in the year but not by any means the only one. On New Year's Eve a big supper was eaten as it was believed that the new year would continue as it began,[49] and in Co. Clare bread was left at the door for the poor on New Year's Day to ensure a blessing of plenty for the year which followed.[50] By St Brighid's Day half the winter stock of food and fuel was supposed to be used up.[51] In the O'Neill land of Co. Armagh apples were saved for St Brighid's Eve to make griddle apple cakes for a festive meal following the making of the St Brighid's Crosses.[52] Shellfish were eaten around Galway on the same day to bring luck to the fishermen for the following year. On other holidays food also played an important part in the festivities, and pancakes were made on Shrove Tuesday when people had their last big meal before the season of fasting. St Patrick's Day was the only day during Lent when people were free to eat and drink their fill, and drowning the shamrock is a tradition established for at least a hundred years. Easter was the occasion of yet another ceremonial meal, when veal or young lamb was eaten. In certain areas a young kid was cooked on this day, and the eating of gaily decorated Easter eggs is an old tradition which may be of pagan origin.[53] The other holiday on which food played an important role was Halloween, or the day before the first day of winter. The usual festive foods were eaten and various games associated with apples, nuts and seasonal foods were played. Barmbrack was eaten and many of the games involved fortune telling by chance; the person who happened to get the ring in a barmbrack would be the first to marry. Nuts were placed by different members of the family on the hearth and those placing them agreed that whichever nut jumped first would indicate the first person to leave home; other divination games were also played.[54] Halloween was a holiday which, though joyful, was tinged with foreboding. It was a time to remember dead relatives and friends, and it was believed to be a time when spirits good and bad were abroad. The long, dark winter was approaching and it was a time when people prepared for the hardship of the winter months.

The formal calendar festivals were not the only occasions when food played a prominent part in the ceremonials of rural Ireland. The first meal from the crop of early potatoes was an occasion of great excitement and a special meal was prepared. A basket of potatoes was dug and with the tender skins peeled or rubbed off they were placed in a three-legged pot and boiled over the open fire. The water was then drained off and the potatoes were mashed using a pounder or beetle. Milk, salt, onions and in some places vegetables or spices were added, and a large hole was made in the middle and filled with butter which melted quickly. The food was then ready for eating. This dish in different varieties was known all over Ireland—in the midlands it was known as *calcannon*, while in Donegal it was *bruitín*. The pecking hens, who were usually given what was left in the pot after meal times, quite often had lean times on days when this dish was served.

In Ulster a match-making cake was baked by the prospective bride's mother and was cut and eaten as soon as the couple agreed on a dowry and the date of the wedding. On summer evenings cake dances were held in many areas,[55] and a Co. Mayo account of this custom which has now disappeared describes how a cake was placed on a pole outside Newport and each dancer paid to join in the dance. Whoever paid most and danced most was presented with the cake.[56] Cake dances were also held on pattern days when different regions celebrated the feast-days of their patron saints. Food and folklore are closely connected in Ireland, and there is an immense amount of oral tradition concerning food—especially the older food items such as milk products and corn.

The local dish is one more aspect of food which cannot be forgotten when viewing the national scene. In the coastal regions cockles, mussels and oysters have always been eaten as well as various types of edible seaweeds. Cockles and mussels were gathered for sale in a few areas, and Mornington outside Drogheda still has its commercial mussel beds, while in Wexford harbour a commercial mussel farm has been introduced in recent years.[57] However, in most areas the beds of cockles and mussels were too small to attract commercial harvesting, although they provided a supplementary food source of great value. It is only in recent years that the oystercatchers have not had to compete with humans in the smaller beds for such non-commercial gastronomic delights. Molluscs and shell-fish were formerly eaten to supplement poor food supplies, but many of these are now popular as delicacies. Periwinkles are sold by street-traders in the towns in Counties Clare, Kerry and Galway and in some of the seaside towns of Northern

Ireland. Shellfish were always plentiful and were eaten in great quantities. Describing this aspect of diet in the Rosses, Co. Donegal, in the year 1788 a clergyman wrote:

'Their shellfish they got in the following manner; the men went to the rocks with a hook tied to the end of a strong rod; and with that they pulled from under the rocks, as many crabs and lobsters as they wanted; the lobsters commonly weighing from five to twelve pounds each: for scollops and oysters, when the tide was out, the younger women waded into the sea where they knew the beds of such fish lay; some of them, naked; others having stripped off their petticoats, went in with their gowns tucked up about their waist; and by armfuls, brought to shore, whatever number of scollops and oysters they thought requisite; the scollops weighing from two to four pounds each.'[58]

In the north *dillisk* or dulse is popular for holidaymakers, and perhaps the most popular of the edible seaweeds is carrageen, which is eaten all over the country and makes excellent jellies, aspics, beverages, blancmanges; it can even be used for making bread and pastry.[59] However, the eating of seaweed was not confined to the poor. The Nugent family of Portaferry House had a silver bowl somewhat like a giant brandy warmer for serving slokum at table.[60] Dried fish, either herring, whiting or ling, was also popular (pl. 77) and indeed rock cod, salted and dried, is still eaten.[61] Originally cured in the kelp ash, it kept indefinitely and was to be seen, during curing, on the roofs of houses. This was then sold inland and was usually hung from the roof rafters. In Donegal it was served with a white sauce made from flour, onions and milk and was often eaten by groups of neighbours who had helped with the hay harvest. Regional food was not confined to coastal regions and local dishes were to be found in many areas. In Co. Cork a distinctive pudding called *drisheen* was made and this was, and indeed still is, much sought after by those who have acquired a taste for it. Traditionally it was made with sheep's blood, but it is now made of pig's blood. This can be purchased still in many shops in the south-west.[62]

The eating habits of the Irish people have gradually changed since the Great Famine. Dependence on the potato declined as the population decreased in numbers and grew in prosperity. Emigration and a new cautious attitude to marriage caused the population to thin out, and the Land Acts in both the late nineteenth and early twentieth centuries made peasant proprietorship the norm. The shock of famine made people avoid dependence on the potato, and so they began to rely more on grain if they could afford to do so. It has been argued that a drop in the price of wheat in the 1860s and 1870s caused by imports from America led to the widespread production of wheaten bread in urban bakeries.[63] This bread became popular in rural areas and many people stopped baking their own bread. In the present century more and more country people began to rely on food supplies purchased from shops, and diet accordingly changed and became more varied. As the bulk of the population left the land and became urban dwellers it seemed inevitable that rural ways would change. Sons and daughters returning from their urban homes and emigrants returning for holidays all became agents of change, and some aspects of traditional fare became associated with poverty and poor life styles.[64] The influences of radio since 1926 and of television since 1960 have also led to further change by graphically illustrating different patterns in many homes. However, many survivals of the old ways are still to be seen, and the meal-bin in which the oatmeal for porridge and the flour for bread were stored can still be seen by the fire in some of the older houses. *Ríobún*, a meal made of freshly ground hardened wheat mixed with morning milk which had been allowed to stand, was popular till recently in Cape Clear. This was regarded as sweeter than warm milk straight from the cow.[65] During the last century American maize, or *yalla male* as it was first known, was distributed as famine relief food. Indeed after the famine it replaced the potato as the staple diet of the labourers who survived,[66] and until recently a few old people still enjoyed an occasional meal of this food. Taste in food changes slowly and it takes strong influences to cause people to abandon traditional eating patterns.

As one German folk-life scholar has written, 'People are nowhere more conservative than in matters relating to mouth and belly.'[67] Changes in eating habits are slow and almost imperceptible, but it seems that the next great change will probably come from outside Ireland as the isolation of nations with regard to food is hopefully nearing an end.

# 6 Transport

Nowadays there is a uniformity about roads and methods of transport which transcends even national boundaries, but not long ago rural Ireland presented a vastly different picture. Roads, which were narrow and gravelled rather than tarred, stretched like veins throughout the country, and horses, ponies and donkeys pulled carts which had the charm of a forgotten age. In mountainous and coastal regions animals with baskets were to be seen, and in some areas block-wheel carts survived long after such primitive vehicles had disappeared from most parts of western Europe. On the bogs, peat—or as it is commonly called in Ireland, turf—is still moved on barrows, sledges and in baskets, and seaweed is still occasionally carried in baskets on the backs of humans and animals. These can now be regarded as survivals of ancient ways and the study of primitive transport is rapidly becoming a matter of historical research rather than of field recording. Tractors have replaced horses and donkeys, while movement to towns and emigration has denuded the countryside of many of its older agricultural population.

The transport of food and fuel is necessary for even the most primitive societies and perhaps the simplest method of porterage is on peoples' backs; there is ample evidence that in Ireland the human beast of burden was much used. The statistical surveys of the early nineteenth century recorded that in Galway baskets were carried by both men and women,[1] while in Monaghan the spreading of manure was also done by carrying loads in back baskets.[2] At the end of the last century Brown remarked on this when he reported on the ethnology of Inishbofin, an island off the Galway coast,[3] and when the photographic era began many examples of people carrying large loads were recorded. As might be expected in trackless areas where carts and even animals could not be taken easily, it was common for people to carry large loads; yet even after the advent of well-metalled roads the old methods survived, for people continued to carry goods on their backs where poverty prevented other methods of transportation. As can be seen from a photograph taken in Connemara in the 1930s it was often the women who carried the heavy loads (pls. 74–5), and there is ample historical evidence to suggest that this was traditionally the case. When Henry Coulter travelled through Ireland in the winter of 1861–2 to examine distress, he reported:

'I have seen more than one poor woman labouring like a horse, toiling backward and forward from the seashore to the field with a heavy load of seaweed, which she had to spread upon the land, whilst her husband performed the much easier task of filling her basket when she returned.'[4]

In the present day people do not often carry heavy loads on their backs, and women rarely carry more than turf into the house for the fire, or other small loads for immediate domestic use.

When large loads were carried the simplest device used was the burden rope. Such ropes are mentioned in the literature of medieval Ireland as items which could be seized by law in settlement of debt,[5] and as such must have been considered to have had some value. These ropes were formerly made from hay, straw, bog wood, rushes, horsehair or other suitable fibrous material and were extensively used for carrying hay, ryegrass, furze, seaweed, rushes, wool, straw, osiers and firewood. Various names were given to these ropes in different regions. In Cork they were known as *iompair ropes*, and in Co. Louth *soogan corn* or *soogan awtha* were the names applied to such items.[6] The method of use was simply to put a loop at one end of the rope, lay the load on the rope, thread the opposite end through the loop, pull it tight and lift it over the shoulder. Burden ropes continued to be used until recently in many areas where either subsistence farming or difficult terrain made their use essential. Back baskets were widely used and were made in almost every part of Ireland. Some were made with shoulder straps of twisted straw and were carried in the same way as modern haversacks; an example from Roscommon made by John Kenny of Newtown for the National Museum is 36 inches high, 29 inches wide and 20 inches broad. This basket, which has an openwork panel 14 inches high in the centre, was used for carrying hay or fodder. Back baskets, however, came in a variety of sizes and shapes and the style varied from district to district and also according to the use for which they were made. For carrying hay or peat a basket with openwork panels to reduce its weight was suitable while, if potatoes or other smaller items had to be carried, a closer weave in the basket was required. When carrying wet loads of seaweed on Aran a sheepskin was first tied to the back, and in some districts back baskets were carried by a single rope which was passed over one shoulder. For small loads baskets with handles were carried in the hand, and old illustrations also show baskets being carried under the arm and resting on the hip. In a country where few manufactured items were in everyday use, baskets were made in a wide variety of shapes and sizes to serve many purposes.

F

In Ireland the custom of carrying goods on the top of a person's head was widespread in many areas until the beginning of this century. In the late 1950s a questionnaire circulated by the Irish Folklore Commission recorded this tradition in all the southern and western counties from Cork to Sligo.[7] It was mainly the women who carried goods on their heads, and the loads carried could be surprisingly large. One informant from Newcastle West, Co. Limerick, recorded in 1957:

'About fifty years ago my mother used to make a ring of her apron, place it on the crown of her head, place a box of butter 56 lbs weight on it and carry it a mile through troublesome country from Killaghteen to Sheehans in Rooska.'[8]

In parts of Co. Clare milk pails, tubs of butter, and baskets of clothes being brought to streams for washing, were carried in this way. Tinsmiths made specially designed containers for carrying water on the head, and in Galway baskets of fish were regularly carried on the tops of women's heads. In other areas the tradition of this method of carrying is less strong, though it is remembered in Waterford, Cavan and Carlow. Fish were brought in baskets carried on women's heads from Lough Neagh to parts of Armagh. This method of porterage is also remembered in Derry while, surprisingly, in neighbouring Donegal there is hardly any trace of such a custom. A pad was placed on the crown of the head to

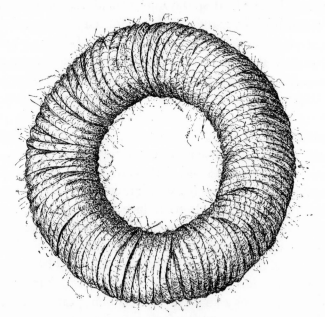

*Fig. 14. A suggan. A hay-rope pad placed on the head by women carrying goods, Kiltoom, Co. Roscommon.*

form a flat platform on which various types of containers could be placed, and this procedure was similar in all areas. In Co. Roscommon this pad, which was known as a *suggan*, was made of twisted hay in the shape of a circle $13\frac{1}{2}$ inches, and $5\frac{1}{2}$ inches in external and internal diameter respectively, and $3\frac{1}{2}$ inches high (fig. 14). This name 'suggan' is generally applied to a straw rope, and in practice it is used for a wide variety of straw objects. In this way liquids such as milk and water could be carried without spilling, fragile items such as eggs could be conveyed without breakages and, from habitual use, the neck muscles were sufficiently developed to enable loads to be carried which to people of today would seem impossible.

From the carrying of goods on people's backs to the carriage of goods on the backs of animals is a small step in the evolutionary scale. The animal most widely used for bearing loads on its back in recent years was the donkey, but horses, ponies and mules were also used extensively as pack animals. As Mahaffy has pointed out, donkeys or asses became popular as beasts of burden in Ireland during the Napoleonic wars when horses were in big demand for campaigns such as that on the Iberian Peninsula.[9]

Donkeys were known in Ireland a long time before 1800 and their bones have been excavated from a crannóg site at Ballydoolough, Co. Fermanagh, which, from the evidence of pot sherds, has been dated to before 1400 BC.[10]

In the early 1960s Michael J. Murphy, while collecting folklore in Co. Louth, discovered an elderly man who remembered his father making a hay-rope pack saddle for carrying turf from a mountain bog in Ravensdale for sale in the town of Dundalk. This pack saddle, one of the simplest methods of securing a load on an animal's back, consisted of a pad of twisted hay in the shape of a long 'U' which lay along the horse's flanks parallel to the spine with the closed end behind the withers (pl. 77). Three cross ties prevented the sides from spreading and a crupper-rope was joined to the open end. Similar pack saddles, sometimes made of oaten straw, have been found in Sligo, Leitrim and Mayo. Lucas, in an article on this pack saddle, showed from documentary evidence that such saddlers were found in Ireland in the seventeenth century and suggested that, along with other items of straw horse harness, these pack saddles may belong to an even earlier date.[11]

The usual method of carrying goods on animals' backs in recent years has been in pairs of baskets or other containers suspended on either side of a wooden pack saddle which usually sits on a mat or pad on the animal's back.[12] The mats were usually of woven straw, and varied in size depending upon the size of the animal, the containers used, and the pack saddle. Some mats were joined permanently to the pack saddle while others were separate. As with many aspects of rural life, especially transport, terminology is a difficulty as pack saddles in Ireland are generically called straddles and are also given local names in different areas. In Donegal the straddle is called a *crutch*, while in Cavan the bow on top of the straddle is called a *crutch*. In the west the name *coirb* is used, while in the south the name *srather fhada* is heard in many areas.

Irish straddles fall into two categories—crook straddles and split straddles. All straddles have two flat boards resting on the mats on the animal's back and the manner of joining these boards is what divides straddles typologically. On the more common crook straddle, these boards are joined by a bow with two upright pegs from which loads are suspended. On split straddles the boards are joined by two boards fitting into one another and the tops of these interlocking horns form hooks from which the baskets are hung. Both crook and split straddles may have one or two pairs of bows or horns, and the connection between the boards on the animal's back was sometimes strengthened by the addition of osier ties. Fenton, in a recent article in which he described Scottish pack saddles, has shown that split straddles have been found in Shetland, Orkney and possibly Caithness, and that they are similar to the split pack straddles found in the Faroe Islands and among the Lapps.[13] Evans has already suggested that split straddles could be of Norwegian origin. In the folk collections of the National Museum of Ireland there is a fine oak split straddle from Cape Clear, Co. Cork. There is also a split straddle with single horns from Carraroe, Co. Galway, while from Cavan and Leitrim there are split straddles with vertical pegs inserted in the same way as such pegs are found in crook straddles. The two straddle types do not follow any clear regional divisions. In Donegal crook straddles with a single bow and two vertical pegs have been found, while in Cavan and Leitrim there are similar straddles as well as split straddles. In Kerry there are single and double bow straddles together with those which have both crook and split straddle features. There are no pegs on some Kerry crook straddles, and the loads were suspended on osier loops attached to the bows. It seems likely that at some stage a strict regional variation in straddles may have existed but in many areas features of both types of straddle can now be found together (figs. 15 and 16).

To secure straddles in position there was always a belly rope and a rope around the animal's tail, usually called a crupper; breast bands to prevent the load from slipping backwards were rarely used. As with burden ropes, these could be made from a wide variety of natural materials, but they were usually made of twisted straw or hay rope. Cruppers were often bound with rags to prevent chaffing under the tail, and the use of wooden crupper boards is also known in Ireland. Crupper ropes were usually fastened to the straddle through holes at the rear of the flat side boards. In other examples the crupper ropes were attached to the bow or to the osier ties between the flat side boards. The belly rope, in some examples, was tied to short

*Fig. 15. Straddle and straw mats, Cullyleenan, Co. Cavan.*

*Fig. 16. Straddle and straw mats, Derryrealt, Co. Cavan.*

osier loops which were laced through holes in the side boards, while in other examples the belly rope was attached to the side board through vertical holes pierced through its width.

A simple rope bridle usually completed the harness. The ingenuity of the countryman and his ability to use the simple materials to be found readily at hand rarely found greater expression than in some of this harness used extensively in all counties well into this century.

The panniers used in pairs on these straddles were known by many names—panniers, baskets, creels, pardogs, keshes and dung pots. Wickerwork baskets were the most popular. D-shaped, square or rectangular sectioned baskets with an openwork panel on the sides were common and many were fitted with a hinged bottom so that the load could be emptied without removing the basket from the animal's back; baskets for animals were similar to those carried on human backs. Photographs show the variety of uses to which animals with straddles were used in the carriage of goods (pl. 78). Water was carried in specially made stave-built containers (pl. 79) and similar containers were probably used in the eighteenth and nineteenth centuries to transport butter from all parts of Munster to the great butter market in Cork. Sand, for agricultural use, was carried in special containers. Evans has illustrated V-shaped wooden creels used for carrying firewood,[14] and Browne recorded similar wooden frames for carrying stones on Clare Island.[15] Though the photographic era arrived too late to record many other uses, it can be assumed that containers were designed to suit a wide range of materials. In recent times baskets have often been replaced by wooden boxes or plastic containers which are easier to obtain as basket-makers, like so many rural craftsmen, become fewer in number.

At the end of the last century Haddon drew attention to the presence in Ireland of the most primitive types of sledges, slide cars and carts.[16] Many scholars have continued this study and it has been acknowledged as one area where it is demonstrably possible to see the past in the present.[17] In the evolutionary scale the change from carrying on an animal's back to using animals to draw loads must have come quickly when it was realized that animals can pull larger loads than they can carry; so the sledge came into being. In Ireland sledges are known by different names in different regions (pl. 82). In Kerry they are called sleighs, in Cork drays, while in the north, as has been pointed out by Thompson, they are known as slipes.[18] A sledge, as described here, is any kind of wheel-less vehicle without shafts used for carrying loads behind an animal. The simple forked branch sledge is found all over Europe,[19] and Ireland is no exception. This consists of a forked branch with some boards attached to form a platform and it is pulled by a draw rope or chain. Sledges were used in recent times when wheeled carts were not practical because of the nature of the terrain. In the prosperous farmland around Dublin sledges were used until recently to remove large stones from fields, but in general sledges survived where the land was poor. In Cork they were used for drawing peat and stones; a Mayo sledge was used for carrying peat and stones, and a box sledge from Co. Fermanagh was used for bringing manure to the fields. All of these have two runners and this is the type of sledge most used in Ireland. In sledges with a box the load was secure, but on flat sledges baskets had to be fitted, especially when bulky loads such as peat were being transported. In Clare sledges with donkeys and traces were regularly used to transport newly cut peat. Finally, Thompson has illustrated single-runner sledges used until the 1950s in Ulster for moving ploughs. A specially designed single-runner iron sledge was also used in Co. Antrim for moving cocks of hay.[20]

Another ancient form of transport found in most parts of the world—the slide car—survived until recently in Ireland (Pl. 80). Edgeworth, writing in 1813, said that slide cars were used in remote parts of Scotland, in the north of Ireland and particularly in Wales.[21] Haddon at the end of the nineteenth century, found slide cars in Antrim, [22] but Evans, in this century, has found them in six of the nine Ulster countries. [23] A slide car from Co. Antrim in the National Museum of Ireland consists of two poles or shafts, four cross bars and two wooden shoes dowelled and secured by two iron ferrules to the ends of the poles. The poles or shafts are 10 feet long and the load-bearing platform is approximately 40 inches wide and 38 inches long. Two vertical mortice holes above the shoes suggest that this car, when in use, had a rod frame to prevent the load falling backwards, or pegs to secure a basket called a *kish*. From photographs taken in the last century we get a good idea of slide cars in use, and in plate 80 the wickerwork basket on a slide car can be seen. Thompson and Evans have both recorded slide cars in use in Co. Antrim as recently as 1948. That wheel-less carts should survive for so long can be attributed to a variety of reasons: slide cars were simple and inexpensive to make, and in some hilly districts they were easier to use than wheeled vehicles; resistance to change and a liking for traditional ways may also have helped to preserve these interesting items.

A cross between a sledge and a wheeled vehicle is found in use on the bogs in Counties Westmeath, Antrim and Sligo. This is called a slipe in the Finea district of Co. Meath and consists of a platform 4 feet long and $2\frac{1}{2}$ feet wide and supported on two wooden rollers with iron axles (pl. 81). The diameter of the rollers is 2 feet, and the slipe is fitted with iron hooks at the sides to which traces are attached when in use. As with so many interesting examples of primitive transport, it is impossible to say whether this is an example of a survival from a pre-wheel culture, or if the rollers were designed to prevent the vehicle sinking in a damp bog. A wide range of wheelbarrows are also found on Irish bogs (pl. 83). These are used for carrying the newly cut sods from the cutting banks to the place where they are laid out to dry. Such barrows have low flat bodies without sides, solid wheels or wheels with spokes and felloes and legs or curved runners which are invariably low. Some barrows have no legs and these vehicles have been compared to the wheeled sledges which are found in Scandinavia and Wales.[24]

One of the earliest pieces of direct evidence of wheeled transport in Ireland was the discovery in a bog in Co. Roscommon in the late 1960s of two massive block wheels dating from about 400 BC.[25] Block wheel is the name given to solid wooden wheels usually constructed from three pieces of timber fastened together with dowels to form a circle. There is ample evidence of similar wheels in use in Ireland until recently though, curiously, some of the ancient wheels were fitted with sleeves to accommodate a fixed axle, while modern block wheels were invariably fitted to an axle which rotated with the wheels. The modern block wheels are therefore more primitive mechanically. The archaeological evidence is too scant to say with certainty what relationship there was between ancient and modern block wheels, and the picture is further complicated by the fact that spoked wheels existed in Ireland from at least the early Christian period and perhaps earlier. A crannóg, excavation at Lough Faughan, Co. Down, produced a spoked wheel from the period AD 600–900,[26] and representations of chariots with spoked wheels appear on some high crosses such as that at Ahenny.[27] Greene has shown that the importance of vehicles as an index of a man's social status was as great in early historic times as modern vehicles are to contemporary society.[28] Though there is ample evidence of roads in medieval Ireland, little is known about the vehicles used on them. Carts and wheels are mentioned in medieval wills, but there is no way of knowing what type of carts or wheels were involved.[29]

From Tudor times the Irish road network began to improve,[30] and the building of the mail-coach roads in the eighteenth century led to the establishment of an integrated network throughout the country. At the same time Grand Juries became actively involved in road building, and most towns were linked by roads which travellers reported to be good for the period. Passenger transport began on a commercial basis, and coach-built vehicles helped to spread the idea of spoked wheels and fixed axles. In the towns coach-builders, wheelwrights and others who serviced this new transport industry made their appearance on the Irish scene.[31]

The nineteenth century saw a revolution in transport. From 1817, famine relief roads brought better communications to mountainous areas of Ireland.[32] Just as Telford's work on the Highland roads and bridges opened up parts of Scotland. The building of a road through the mountains from Macroom to Glenflesk shortened the distance from Kenmare, Co. Kerry to Cork by 31 statute miles.[33] Achill and areas around Crookhaven, previously inaccessible to wheeled vehicles, were joined by new roads to neighbouring towns.[34] Wheeled carts made their first appearance in modern times in some districts, and the folklore archives record that in Ballintra, Co. Donegal, wheelwrights from Fifeshire brought over and introduced spoked wheels for the first time in the 1820s.[35] Here documentary evidence and oral tradition are in agreement as J. Hamilton in his memoirs recorded the introduction of Scottish wheelwrights in the Brown Hall Estate in Donegal in 1823.[36] However, the transport revolution was not confined to roads and vehicles, and many canals were built in the eighteenth century, railway building began in 1834, and by 1870 all the main lines were completed.

The fashion of the eighteenth and nineteenth centuries made travel a necessity for those who could afford it and parts of Ireland became popular tourist paths. Many descriptive works were written, and block-wheel carts were widely commented on as they contrasted sharply with vehicles in use in other countries, even though such wheels were known in other parts of Europe and Asia.[37] The modern block-wheel cart had an axle which rotated with the wheel (pl. 84) and below each shaft there was normally a block of wood with the lower surface curved to accommodate the axle on which it rested. In modern examples the axle is kept in place beneath the shafts by two semi-circular iron hoops bolted to this block of wood;[38] these hoops do not fit tightly but rather allow the axle to rotate freely. When in use it was necessary to lubricate these contact points frequently as the friction was great. The weight of the solid wheels prevented large wheels being used when the cart was being drawn by a single animal and consequently the shafts and floor of the carts sloped sharply backwards when being drawn by an average-sized horse. This tended to tip the load off and, to overcome this, low creels were added to the back and sides. As these tapered in height to the front, the result was that the top of these low creels formed a horizontal platform and, in some later carts, this was converted into the floor of the cart. The shafts of block-wheel carts were attached to the axle inside the wheels of some carts and outside in others, and contemporary illustrations show that few regional patterns for 'inside' and 'outside' carts are discernible. The cross beams between the shafts making up the floor of the cart were known in Galway as laces, and in many of the block-wheel carts there were four of these. In recent times the word lace is used to describe the boards on top of the shafts forming the body of the cart, and in Offaly a cart known as a 'four lace cart' had a rectangular frame of four boards which held a wickerwork basket 64 inches long by 51 inches wide by 25 inches deep.

Block-wheel carts were used extensively for carrying passengers and the jaunting car or side car developed from this cart. Croker's illustration of 1824 shows people sitting on a block-wheel cart,[39] and this cart was improved upon more and more until the side car, with space for passengers to sit back to back with their feet over the wheels of this lightweight vehicle with spoked wheels, was evolved. This car is still very popular in areas of high tourist interest like Killarney and Aran where many are still in use. Haddon, who traced the development of the side car or jaunting car in the early nineteenth century, quoted what one traveller wrote in 1834:

'Although there are carriages of all descriptions in Ireland and coaches, too, on many of the principal roads, the jaunting car is the national vehicle and Ireland would scarcely be Ireland without it. It may be said to completely supersede as a private vehicle the whole of the gig tribe—dennet, tilbury, cabriolet, etc.—and to be a formidable rival to the coach as a public conveyance.'[40]

Charles Bianconi, the most successful organizer of a passenger transport system on the Irish roads before the famine in the 1840s, developed his own 'long cart' on the lines of the jaunting car.[41] Bianconi's long cars were capable of carrying up to sixteen persons and, with 1300 horses in service, he had more horses than the British army in Ireland. Jaunting cars and long cars were gradually improved and by the end of the nineteenth century they had sophisticated springs, hickory shafts and pneumatic tyres[42] (pl. 85). The advent of the motor car and mechanized public transport has ended people's dependence on horse-drawn vehicles, and they are rarely to be seen now except as items of historic interest for the amusement of tourists or enthusiasts.

In the Irish countryside the carriage of goods was always of greater interest than passenger transport, as people were accustomed to walking great distances or going on horseback. Just as the Scotch plough was introduced into Ireland so also was the Scotch cart, which made its way to this country across the narrow straits from our closest neighbours. R. L. Edgeworth described the Scotch cart in 1813 as having wheels about 4 feet high and hardly any sides or ends, and so it was very light[43] (fig. 17). From Edgeworth's sketches we can get an idea of both the Scotch cart and contemporary block-wheel carts. Despite the fact that many argued the doubtful superiority of block-wheel native carts, the Scots cart which had a fixed iron axle, made rapid progress in Ireland; these carts could carry loads twice the weight of those carried in block-wheel carts. During the Napoleonic wars the Scotch cart became popular in northern parts of the country where they were extensively used for agricultural purposes and for carrying linen.[44] From the northern counties Scotch carts spread rapidly to other areas until they were to be seen all over the country. A feature of these early Scotch carts was the flat body with long projecting rear shafts which are called trams in some areas (pl. 86). The flat body contrasted with the low backs of the block-wheel carts, which gave the name

*Fig. 17. Irish carts, c. 1800. After Edgeworth.*

'low-backed cars' to Irish vehicles with small wheels. The rear shafts, which prevent the cart tipping too far back during unloading, may be reminiscent of the long slide-car runners, as has been suggested.[45] Green, however, has shown that these features were known on Irish vehicles in early historic times, and similar rear shafts were found in the Low Countries and in France.[46] Rear shafts, which are necessary for the easy and safe handling of a cart when the horse is unyoked, should probably be regarded as functional items and not as indications of cultural survivals of earlier vehicles.

During the nineteenth century the Scotch cart developed, and the most obvious change was the introduction of the box which was sometimes removable to give a flat cart again. The flat cart with long rear shafts survived longest in the west and the south, while in Leinster and Ulster the improved box cart with its solid sides and tail board was more popular. Both flat carts and box carts had provision for additional creels for use when carrying peat or other light bulky loads, or when carrying animals. The improved Scotch cart was especially favoured by Leinster farmers for transporting sacks of grain. These carts when so loaded put considerable strain on horses when going downhill, and in the Leixlip area near Dublin a brake, consisting of a heavy iron shoe with a roller at the front, was placed under one wheel (pl. 88). This had the effect of making the cart into a kind of semi-slide cart while the shoe was in position, and this form of brake was in use until recently. Similar brakes were used on the mail coaches in the eighteenth century, and this is one example of how change and adaptation took place. Many other adaptations of the Scotch cart took place. In Dublin and Wexford a cart was designed in which the shafts were hinged to the body of the cart so that it could tip up without unharnessing the animal, and in other areas distinctive outward-curving guard rails were placed over the wheels. In many places light flat carts and heavy box carts were found together, each being used for the purpose for which it was best suited.

Although a few examples of the English farm waggon have been recorded,[47] it never became popular and Ireland basically remained an area in which only two-wheeled carts were in widespread use. In the cities and towns four-wheeled drays were common at the beginning of the present century, but four-wheeled vehicles never invaded rural Ireland

The horse- or donkey-drawn cart gave enormous service to Irish country people. It could be used for bringing home the produce of the land; fitted with special creels it could transport a large amount of peat for winter warmth and, if poverty prevented the purchase of a jaunting car or trap, it could be used on shopping expeditions to the towns and villages. In the towns, shops, hotels and public houses had provision in their yards for stabling the horse or donkey while its owner promenaded the town, or enjoyed the hospitality of the house. On fair days and market days most country towns were invaded by hundreds of carts, traps and other vehicles. In recent years the buying and selling of animals has moved off the streets and market squares to highly organized marts where animals are auctioned, and fairs and markets, where they survive, tend to follow a different pattern. New agricultural methods, the growth of relative prosperity and changing patterns of rural life have almost brought down the final curtain on primitive transport in Ireland (pl. 87).

# 7 The Year's Work

Man's principal activity in rural Ireland has always been agriculture and the various tasks associated with farming. Indeed it is only in the last decade that the balance in Irish society has changed, and now the majority of the population live in urban areas. Up to the 1960s the Irish were mainly rural dwellers and even in the towns and villages the connections with the country were binding and strong. In the past the year's work for rural dwellers mainly involved securing their requirements for food, shelter and warmth. Most farmers attended their own crops, built their own houses, herded their own cattle, sheep and other animals and cut their own peat. The womenfolk were often equally engaged in these tasks, and added to them the making and repairing of clothes and cooking the family's food. Rural craftsmen were engaged in similar activities and the country weaver usually farmed his own plot of land. Even though a money economy has operated in most parts of Ireland for centuries, rural dwellers regarded self-sufficiency as normal and earnings were often only needed for the payment of rents, taxes and tithes. Many writers have remarked upon the Irishman's attachment to the land and when the history of the country is examined this is hardly surprising. The fortunes of families usually depended on the produce of the land, and only in the present century has the economy been diversified and the proportionate numbers engaged in agriculture decreased. In viewing life and tradition in rural Ireland the plough field and pasture are as important as the battlefield in charting the fortunes of ordinary countryfolk (pl. 90).

The pastoral side of agriculture was certainly most important in earliest times, but crop cultivation took place almost from the beginning of settlement in Ireland. Recent excavations in Mayo have uncovered regular field patterns with a house site and a court cairn burial site which pre-date the bog which now blankets the whole area. These regular fields have been dated from the period 1000 BC to 300 BC.[1] Clearance and enclosure were common in the upland forest areas in the Neolithic and Bronze Ages; the Celts began a new era and introduced new field systems and clearance in lowland areas. Common ownership and use of these fields was the norm, and this indigenous field system later developed in many areas into the so-called rundale system with infield cultivation and grazing usually restricted to the unenclosed common land. In some areas unenclosed land could still be seen until recently and the Irish Land Commission has, in the past forty years, had the task of dividing up land held in common from time immemorial.

The turbulent history of Ireland has had its effect on even the common fields, and the Normans introduced the manorial system which contrasted dramatically with the older patterns. This had to be adapted initially to the existing field systems, but gradually the new distribution with parcels of land for different social groups became common. Three-yearly crop rotation on the manorial farms led to further enclosure in the period 1171–1300. The manor often became the nucleus of a village settlement, and while some of the lower orders lived in separate areas in the older style, the manors gave parts of Ireland a distinctive landscape.[2] The Tudor–Stuart plantations continued the process of enclosure and the establishment of rural villages. The second half of the eighteenth century was the last great period of enclosure and in the early nineteenth century the continuous subdivision of farms led to the creation of a patchwork of tiny fields in many parts of the country. Today progressive farmers are consolidating holdings and amalgamating fields to enable the use of larger machinery and to increase the area of cultivation. In the past fences and ditches took various forms and as Evans has demonstrated some of these can be dated by the style of construction.[3] Techniques of building have remained the same in many areas over a long period, and the dry stone walls built in recent years in many parts of the south and west vary very little from the type of walls built in Neolithic times; indeed, some field walls may originally have been built then (pl. 89). Fields and fences in rural Ireland breathe history, much of life and tradition relates to the landscape so created and the year's work often involved being in the fields.

The importance of cattle in rural Ireland in almost all periods meant that the year's work was closely associated with their care and herding. Throughout the ages cattle have been both the prime suppliers of food and the chief form of wealth and they are known to have existed in Ireland from Neolithic times.[4] Now, only the small breed of Kerry cows remain as survivors of the pre-medieval Irish cattle types, and even they are in danger as there are only a couple of hundred left in Ireland. The records of the early historic period speak continuously of cattle—Irish society in the medieval period was based more on pastoralism than on agriculture, and stock raising was more important than tillage. The care of cattle was the concern of the whole family, and cattle raiding was a permanent aspect of rural life until the restructuring of rural society in the seventeenth century. The early

Irish epic poems describe these raids, and the annals record occasions when over a thousand animals were captured in a single raid.[5] To understand this society it is necessary to compare it with pastoral societies which have survived into modern times mainly in Third World countries. One aspect of this pastoral life was the removal of some of the herds to summer pastures in the hills. Though medieval records tell little of this a picture of how it operated can be reconstructed from oral accounts from areas where it survived into the present century.[6] The best of these accounts was recorded by Seán Ó'hEochaidh of the Irish Folklore Commission from a Donegal man called Niall Ó'Dubhthaigh who was born on 9 April 1874. He recalled how his mother described the fun and pleasure she had in her youth when she and the daughters of three other families took the animals to the hill pastures from May to October. Significantly the terminal days are celebrated in two feast-days—May Day and All Hallows—which were festive days even before Christianity. The men went up first and built the huts which were to be the girls' homes. These were sometimes large enough to accommodate a sick animal and were usually made of sod in a dry spot near a stream. Sheepskins were used for the windows, and heather was strewn on the floors which were made of blue clay. The girls' time on the hills was fully occupied for besides tending the flocks they also made butter, grew potatoes, carded wool, knitted socks and generally worked hard. Yet the booley huts, as such huts were called, were regarded as places of pleasure, and occasional nights of singing and dancing took place,[7] when boys from the home villages visited. Transhumance, as this custom was called, was well known in Europe[8] and, although it died out in the last century, there is widespread evidence that it once was common in many parts of Ireland. There are remains of booley huts on many hills, and in the valley of the King's river in Co. Wicklow the remains of a cluster of six can be seen at a height of 1120 feet above sea level in the townland of Garryknock. All that can be seen on the ground is the foundation of the oval and circular huts, and it would be interesting to know more of this aspect of life. Excavation of more sites of this kind might increase our knowledge of the year's work in the past in rural Ireland. From the mountain booleys of old to the mechanized milking stalls of the present the tending of cattle has remained a constant facet of the year's work.

The people of the cashel, ringfort and crannóg were primarily pastorialists yet they knew, as did their predecessors, the skills and techniques of growing farinaceous crops.[9] The excavations in north-west Mayo have shown that cultivation in ridges was common even among the earliest settlers. Our knowledge of the tools used by these settlers is limited. Only plough pebbles,[10] shares and coulters of ploughs have been found in the period up to AD 1600. Ploughs were used in all

74. *Connemara man and woman* (B.F. TY91).

75. *Woman carrying turf, Connemara* (B.F. TY237).

76. *Bringing home hay, Connemara* (N.M.I. SF241).

77. *Hay-rope straddle*
*(N.M.I. F1961: 84).*

78. *Straddle with baskets for kelp,*
*Aran Islands, Co. Galway*
*(B.F. TY151).*

79. *Water carriers (B.F. TY82).*

80. *Slide car, block-wheel cart and Scots
cart, Glenshesk, Co. Antrim
(N.L.I. R3498).*

81. *Turf slipe, Co. Sligo (N.M.I. SF257).*

82. Below: *Sledge, Co. Dublin
(N.M.I. DF319).*

83. Below right: *Turf barrow,
Boherbree, Co. Kildare.*

84. *Block-wheel cart near Athlone, Co. Westmeath, 1811. From* R. H. *Newell,* Poetical Works of Oliver Goldsmith (*London, 1811*).

85. *Jaunting car* (N.L.I. 2562WL).

86. *Carts in line at creamery, Co. Limerick* (B.F. TY77).

87. *Bringing home the hay on a bogey,*
*Co. Dublin* (B.F. TY55).

88. *Brake for Scots cart, Leixlip,*
*Co. Kildare.*

89. *Stone walls, west Cork.*

90. *Making ridges, Aran Islands*
(B.F. TY*157*).

91. *Tomb of Alexander Black*
*erected 1826 in Skreen, Co. Sligo*
(N.M.I. DF*2124*).

92. *Wooden plough, Kinvarra, Co.*
*Galway* (N.M.I. DF*394*).

93. *Turf-cutting, Rosmuc, Co. Galway (B.F. TY289A).*

94. *Irish spades.*

95. *Wooden-iron plough, north Co. Dublin.*

96. *Reaping with sickle* (N.M.I. *CF332*).

97. *Reaping with scythe* (B.F. *TY45*).

98. *Reaper and binder, Ardmore, Co. Waterford* (B.F. *TY179*).

99. Below: *Horse-powered thresher, Co. Kerry* (B.F. *TY205*).

100. *Drum of horse-powered thresher, Co. Galway* (B.F. TY56).

101. *Threshing mill, Co. Cavan* (B.F. TY41).

102. *Threshing day, Killarney, Co. Kerry* (B.F. TY54/48).

103. Below: *Mowing machine, Co. Donegal* (B.F. TY43).

*104. 'Tumbling Paddy' in use at Ballysokerry, Co. Mayo* (B.F. TY47/48).

*105. Corn stacks on stone stands near Athenry, Co. Galway* (N.M.I. DF3235).

*106. Haymaking near Lisdoonvarna, Co. Clare* (B.F. TY40/48).

*107. Haycock lifter* (N.M.I. CF*164*).

*108. Sheep-shearing, Aran Islands, Co. Galway* (B.F. TY*149*).

*109. Sheep-shearing* (B.F. TY*12/53*).

110. *Fair day, Killarney, Co. Kerry* (N.L.I. *3549WL*).

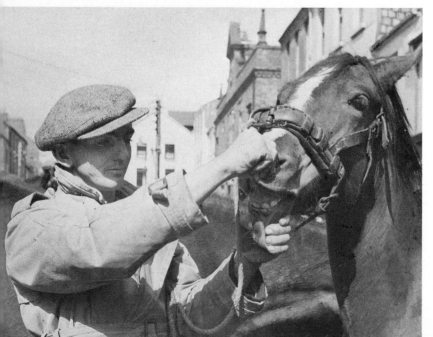

111. *Inspecting horse's teeth, Killarney, Co. Kerry* (B.F. TY*20/50*).

*112. Collecting seaweed* (B.F. TY203).

*113. Collecting seaweed, Aran Islands, Co. Galway* (B.F. TY158).

*114. Burning kelp, Aran Islands, Co. Galway* (N.M.I. CF229).

115. *Cutting and gathering seaweed* (B.F. TY57).

116. *Boat-load of seaweed* (B.F. TY273).

117. *Building a seaweed raft, Rosaveel, Connemara.*

118. *Poling a seaweed raft, Ballinderreen, Co. Galway.*

119. *Baiting spillet lines, Tory Island* (N.M.I. CF474).

*120. Dragnetting, Aran Islands, Co. Galway (B.F. TY144).*

*121. Seine net in use. Detail of part of Boyne fishermen's trade union banner.*

*122. Drying mackerel, Aran Islands, Co. Galway (B.F. TY73).*

periods and Lucas has ably described ploughing practices in different periods.[11] The ox was the universal draught animal down to the twelfth century when the horse began to be used, and by the sixteenth century the horse was the usual draught animal for ploughing. Though no complete Irish prehistoric or medieval ploughs have been found it is certain that they were crude and much less effective than those introduced later. The method of harnessing the oxen—there were usually two to six used at any one time—was to tie up the plough to a wooden yoke by means of ropes made of timber withies, straw, rushes or even horsehair. Another method which both Lucas and Evans have described was to attach the plough to the horse's tail. By the sixteenth century English ploughs were being introduced in parts of Gaelic Ireland and this trend continued until in the eighteenth century pamphlets began to appear praising the increased efficiency of the new types of ploughs.[12] By 1770 the Dublin Society was encouraging experiments in agriculture and the manufacture of a wide range of new agricultural implements[13] began in small factories such as the one at Celbridge.[14] The dramatic improvements in ploughs in Scotland at the same time were to have rapid consequences in Ireland, and the greater availability of iron made it easier for such ploughs to be made (pl. 91). Statistical surveys of the early nineteenth century show how rapidly the new Scotch ploughs were introduced, and throughout the country many small factories were set up. In Dublin Le Strange, Paul and Vincent, Sheridan, Kennedy and Graham were all manufacturing their own machines while Drummonds and Keenans were agents for British manufacturers.[15] Ploughs made by many of these can still be seen in the Leinster area with the makers' names stamped on the top of the beam and in Kilkenny, Wexford and other areas the picture was similar; Pierce's of Wexford made, and still make, ploughs which were very popular. Side by side with iron ploughs, wooden ploughs were also made and are obviously modelled on the improved Scotch plough. Wooden ploughs were still made in parts of Co. Galway until the 1950s (pl. 98), and even now small ploughs pulled by donkeys can still be seen in gardens in parts of Co. Clare and even around Dublin (pl. 95).

Although the plough was used in all ages, the spade was the universal implement used for cultivation by the common labourer in Ireland. From earliest times down to the present day the spade has had a special place in Irish rural life.[16] The earliest farmers used spades to build ridges on which to grow their crops, and the potato ridges still used in the west of Ireland are the same as those earlier models. The landscape is littered with reminders of spade cultivation, and the outline of such ridges, usually called lazy-beds, can be seen clearly on hillsides where the land is no longer regarded as suitable for cultivation. The spade was the essential tool of the trade of the wandering labourer in the eighteenth and nineteenth centuries. The hiring fair where agricultural labourers were selected by farmers was a feature of Irish rural life until the 1930s. My friend Patrick Campbell has described his experience of going from his home on the Croagh Gorm mountain to the Diamond in Donegal for his first hiring in 1926.[17] At the age of fifteen many boys from the western counties went to work in the more prosperous parts of the country from May to November, first as servant boys, and later as ploughmen, dairymen, turfcutters and harvesters.[18] It is difficult to describe the amount of mobility in rural Ireland in all periods because of its extent and complexity. In the medieval period the great herds of cattle had to be followed, and the booleys brought the people to the hills. In the same period and earlier, wandering scholars, clerics and poets roamed the roads of Europe 'putting up learning for sale in the markets and often vexing the souls of bishops with strange heresies and doctrines unknown to the councils of the church'.[19] This aspect of medieval society is shadowy and difficult to reconstruct, for much of it was destroyed in the crises of the seventeenth century only to re-emerge in the next hundred years in a different form. Wandering schoolmasters, poets and musicians were the successors of this cultural aspect of the destroyed medieval world.[20] However, not all the wanderers were scholars or labourers, and the wandering poor increased in numbers in every succeeding generation before the Great Famine;[21] tinsmiths, tailors and stonemasons also joined in to swell the numbers of the mobile population. These were the people who often kept the oral tradition alive in Ireland, and many a *spailpín* or wandering labourer was also a poet, storyteller or entertainer. In describing the year's work this aspect of rural life should be remembered.

The actual spades used by the rural population have been thoroughly described. From the wooden iron-shod spades of the late Christian period to spades and turf slanes of the modern period there are such regional variations that it is almost possible to tell a spade's place of origin from its size and form (pl. 94). The Munster spades had long narrow blades with fishtail ends while in Connaught the blade was shorter and broader. In Sligo, Longford and Cavan the peculiar big loy was favoured and in other areas it was said that a person's religious beliefs could be determined by the foot with which he dug. It is interesting to see what has made it possible to study the spade in such detail. Originally almost all implements were made by local blacksmiths who designed spades to suit local conditions, uses and preferences. When the manufacture was taken over by spade mills, the millwrights copied the local types in order to compete for customers, and many spade mills continued to make hundreds of different types until well into the present century. A large spade mill near Clonskea Bridge in Dublin still had its patterns when it closed within the last twenty years, and the spades were aquired by the folk life division of the National Museum. The Northern Ireland Folk Museum were also fortunate in getting not only regional patterns but also actually moving an old mill into its grounds at Cultra where the knowledgeable spade-maker is able to continue his craft. From these valuable collections detailed studies of this key feature of rural life have been possible.[22]

The spade was only one of a wide variety of hand tools used in the fields and gardens. The flatcher or breast-plough was popular in northern counties,[23] and the mattock is still used in small gardens in west Cork where it was once very popular. Jack 'Rick' O'Donovan still uses one, called a *graffan*, to prepare my garden for potatoes and vegetables at Lonagh; thistle thongs with both iron and wooden heads were used in every area (fig. 18). Many tools were designed to do specific jobs. Furze lifters were heavy iron implements consisting of V-shaped prongs with a bow at the back and a long wooden handle; the prongs were driven under the furze, and the handle was used as a lever to raise the bush. There were special tools for pounding the bush[24] afterwards, and it was then used extensively as fodder. A smaller variety of this tool was used for lifting dock weeds, and for peat or turf cutting there was a special spade called a slane. Peat, which has always been important as fuel in Ireland (up to eight million tons were cut by hand in 1920), has again become popular in recent years as other types of fuel have become expensive.[25] People also burned timber from the bogs. This was located by a long iron probe and bog wood was widely used for making ropes, for fuel, for roof timbers, for making furniture and for carving ornaments which were very popular at the end of the last century.[26] The list of such specialized tools is endless as each job created its own demands, and as long as the country blacksmith was the maker each implement was made to suit not only the demands of the job, but also the physique and temperament of the user.

Change took place, however, and after the Great Famine farms grew larger and more and more people turned to the use of the horse on the farm. The rate of change varied from place to place and on the small farms in the west it was least noticeable. The sickle was used for reaping in Ireland from earliest times as the archaeological evidence shows. Country blacksmiths made sickles to a roughly similar pattern, and even today sickles made in eastern Europe are sold in Irish shops (pl. 96). The sickle was gradually replaced by the scythe (pl. 97) and in areas in the east and south a distinctive bow was added when reaping corn so as to leave it in bundles ready for tying in sheaves. Similar bows can be seen in sixteenth-century Dutch paintings, and are still occasionally used in parts of Co. Offaly. Both sickle and scythe gradually gave way to reapers and binders which in their

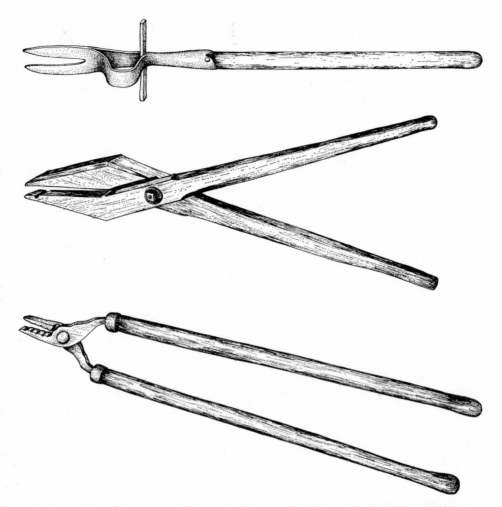

*Fig. 18. Farmer's hand implements.* Top: *Dock digger, Red Cross, Co. Wicklow.* Middle: *Wooden thistle tongs, Temple Michael, Co. Longford.* Bottom: *Thistle tongs, Hollywood, Co. Dublin.*

day were impressive pieces of technology (pl. 98). In the same way horse-powered threshing machines replaced flails and Pierce's of Wexford produced effective, if primitive, machines at the turn of the century (pls. 99–100). Steam-powered threshers were used for a short time, and from the 1930s threshing machines made by the famous English manufacturers gradually became more popular as tractors were introduced to some farms (pls. 101–2); since the 1960s combine harvesters have made even these obsolete. The saving of hay also changed with the introduction of mowing machines and a wide variety of horse-drawn rakes (pl. 103).

Perhaps the most popular of these was the American-designed machine known as the 'Tumbling Paddy' which consisted simply of a beam with a row of spikes on either side (pl. 104).[27] When sufficient hay was gathered the operator rotated the beam of lifting the handle, and this left the hay in neat rows for drying and for building into cocks later. Indeed hay is no longer saved as in the past, and more and more farmers are turning to silage as an alternative. The great rick of hay in the vicinity of large farmhouses is a thing of the past and it has been replaced with silage pits (pl. 114). Similarly the great stacks of corn have disappeared—and in some places the straw is burned in the fields. The stones on which such stacks were built in many areas stand like mute reminders of an age which has just passed (pl. 105). This picture of change in methods of production can be seen in photographs taken in the early years of this century. The old Aran man clipping with scissors contrasts with the hand-powered shearing machine which in turn is now obsolete (pls. 108–9). Although in the 1930s the hand-cranked cock lifter was a symbol of progress, this and all the horse-powered machines are now gone from Irish farms and the year's work is now vastly changed (pl. 107). Not only have the implements of agriculture changed but so also have many of the older habits, and with modern machinery it is not as necessary for farmers to depend upon neighbours. A *meitheal* or voluntary gathering of neighbours for threshing, haymaking or other major tasks is not essential nowadays, and with rural depopulation in many areas it is no longer possible. So many of the most joyful occasions in rural Ireland have disappeared, but perhaps the ability to judge the value of an animal remains as a permanent asset to the contemporary farmer (pl. 110). Even the ritual hand slapping and bargaining at country fairs has now moved to newly built auction marts where the business remains the same, but the ceremonial is abandoned in favour of the sterile ways of strict commerce.

The year's work varied from person to person. On the coast many rural dwellers were occupied harvesting the sea and the shore for food and useful materials. Seaweed was collected for eating, for burning to make kelp and for manuring the potato fields (pls. 112–4). It was collected in baskets at low tide, it was cut with knives at the end of long poles by men standing in boats (pl. 115) and floating seaweed was taken from the sea in nets held by men who waded into the breakers.[28] Great loads of seaweed were carried in boats (pl. 116) which were punted as rafts along the coast (pls. 117–18), and from the shoreline people collected periwinkles, cockles, mussels, crab, lobster and crayfish. In the shallow water in Clonakilty Bay, Co. Cork, people can still occasionally be seen catching sand eels using old billhooks to throw them in the air before catching them in buckets.[29] Fishing is of course a major part of the year's work for many rural dwellers in coastal regions, and although in the past a wide variety of traditional methods were used, these have now largely disappeared. Weirs or traps made from osiers or stone for catching salmon in estuaries are no longer made, and the osier lobster pots have given way to modern French manufactured examples. Seine netting, which was popular in both estuaries and on the coast, is no longer practised (pls. 120–1). Line fishing from small boats using a spillet or basket to carry a number of lines is not carried on commercially now, and in-shore fishermen in Ireland have become comparable to their colleagues on the Scottish or French coasts (pl. 119). The commercial fishing of the 25-foot-long basking shark has declined, although for more than two hundred years fishermen in small boats caught these giant fish off the coasts of Mayo and Galway. In the past the sun fish, as these were called, were important to the local economy in some areas.[30] Now shark are more important as a fish to be caught by sportsmen and this is the centre of a new type of tourist activity. Such fishing has little to do with traditional ways when sun fish were chased for necessity not pleasure, or the old ways which were so accurately recorded in Robert Flaherty's film *Man of Aran*. The rich bounty of the sea was always used, though shortage of sophisticated equipment prevented intensive exploitation in any period.

In any comment on the year's work in rural Ireland the country crafts deserve mention. Although the country people were largely self-sufficient they depended for many articles upon the expertise of the craftsman. The poverty of the country probably meant that most craftsmen were paid in kind and were usually part-time farmers as well; yet the number of people listed as craftsmen in the early census reports gives an idea of just how many of these there were. In Co. Clare in 1831 there were 1188 weavers, 632 tailors and breeches makers, 610 shoe and boot makers or menders, 547 blacksmiths or horse shoers, 515 carpenters, 322 masons or wallers, 182 coopers, 164 butchers or fleshers, 104 nailers and besides these a host of other trades and crafts were recorded. These included bakers (64), basket makers (6), besom makers (5), boat builders (28), book binders (2), brass workers or tinkers (38), brewers (4), brogue makers (72), builders of various kinds (54), slaters (59), cabinet makers (11), sawyers (83), wheelwrights (59), carriers or carters (51), cart makers (20), chemists (19), clock makers (5), clothiers (32), curriers (9), cutlers (4), drysalters (7), dyers (23), farriers or cow doctors (8), feather dressers (34), flax dressers (21), glaziers or plumbers (20), glovers (8), gun makers (3), harness makers or collar makers (24), hatters or hosiers (65), jewellers (4), maltsters (3), marble cutter (1), millers (41), millwrights (4), nailers (104), scavengers or nightmen (7), paper makers (6), cooks (12), pawnbrokers (10), printers (14), saddlers (25), soot and chimney sweepers (10), spirit merchants (54), stone cutters

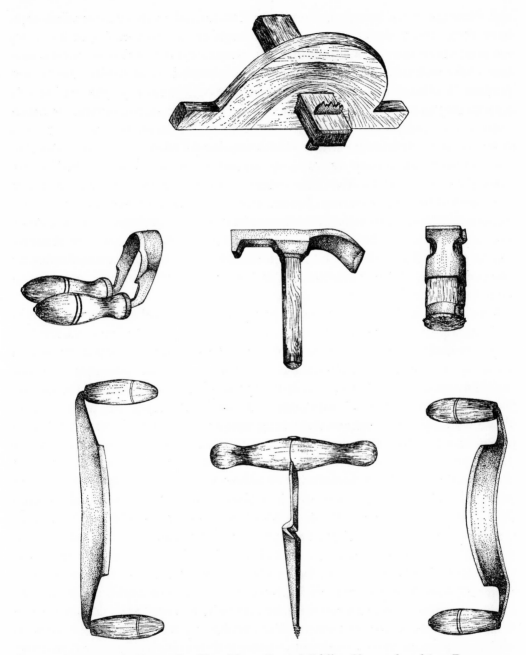

*Fig. 19. Cooper's tools, Ennis, Co. Clare.* Top: *Croze.* Middle: *Shave, adze, driver.* Bottom: *Drawing knife, toper auger, hollowing knife.*

(24), straw plait and bonnet makers (6), tallow chandlers or wax chandlers (15), tanners (12), thatchers (9), tinmen (20), tobacconists (13), toymen (3), turners (13), one upholsterer and one whitesmith.[31] Some of these were obviously trades rather than crafts and it is interesting to note the occupations attracting the largest numbers. The largest numbers of craftsmen were engaged in supplying basic needs of food, shelter and clothing. Even though the trades listed here include the urban craftsmen in Clare, it can be seen that agriculture dominated society in the nineteenth century. The list presents some interesting problems. Why were there so few thatchers in a county where most houses would have had thatched roofs? The answer must be that thatching except in a few cases was not regarded as a specialist task or a full-time occupation. The high number of slaters is surprising, but this can be explained by the existence in east Clare of a slate works and the popularity of slates in the country towns; the large number of coopers were necessary to supply the needs of the butter trade. Many country crafts are, it must be assumed, under-represented in this list and many are now but vague memories in rural Ireland.

The 104 nailers in Co. Clare must have provided a useful service to remain in business. But how many people now know what they did? As the name implies, they provided nails they made themselves and also a number of other items like pig-rings. The nailer's forge resembled the blacksmith's; he heated the thin iron bar on a fire with a bellows, beat it to a point on an anvil, cut out the desired length, placed it in a 'nailer's tool', turned the projecting top and beat it to a head. Those who had the privilege of watching such craftsmen have all commented on the speed with which they worked, producing nails with lightning movements of their hands. Some even had trip hammers in their workshops to increase the speed of production. The invention of mass-produced wire nails brought the craft to an end and families like the Samways in Galway, the Currans in Loughrea, McCulloughs in Longford, the Bairds in Warrenpoint and Tohalls in Tyrone were all forced out of their ancestral businesses.[32] Hand-made nails, which can be seen in many old buildings, will no longer be made and the skill of the craft is lost for ever.

The nailer is not the only craftsman who has been threatened or driven out of business. The tinsmith with his interesting collection of traditional tools and methods of manufacture survives, but he cannot be regarded as a craftsman with a great future (pls. 123–4).[33] Country blacksmiths and wheelwrights still cling to precarious existences (pls. 125–6) and spinning and weaving have almost completely disappeared (pl. 127). Where once every parish had a weaver, now weaving is rarely found as a country craft and the allied skills of spinning, thickening and napping have disappeared. Even where linen is made in the northern counties the method of manufacture is much different to that described and illustrated by Hinks in his eighteenth-century prints. In the old days flax was sown in April and pulled in July and the seed was removed using a ripple. The flax was then bound in sheaves with rushes and steeped in ponds of soft water where the softer tissues disintegrated and the hard fibres remained. It was next dried and then the scutching followed. In the scutching the boon or remaining non-fibrous portion was beaten away, leaving the pure fibre (pl. 128). This was then hackled in the same way as wool, spun into yarn and woven into linen. Old scutching mills with their works intact can still be seen even in areas like Co. Cavan where flax is no longer widely grown (pl. 130).[34] Similarly, scutching boards, blades and other old tools connected with the linen trade can be found in houses where the craft is long forgotten. Of the craftsmen of former years few now remain. The carpenter is still found (pl. 129), but the old wood-turners with their pole lathes are gone (pl. 131),[35] the water diviner with his strange magical hazel stick has still to be replaced by modern technology as a guide to sources of water and a few blacksmiths still flourish, but the great variety and mass of craftsmen are gone and many have vanished unrecorded. What a pity that more of these had not the education, interest or ability of Seamus Murphy, who recorded with wit and accuracy his experiences as a wandering stone-mason.[36] The country craftsmen were essential in most rural communities where they brought specialist skills greater than the countryman's own. The craftsmen and the countrymen of old exploited all the resources of the land to mutually sustain themselves and this aspect of the struggle for existence is well expressed in the poem 'The Last Will and testament of a dying male' written by an anonymous country poet or rhymer from Killoughy, Co. Offaly.

> *I leave my flesh unto the dogs, for thats their precious right,*
> *I will my bowels and entrails to the eagle, hawk and kite,*
> *To every honest claimant I wish to do what's fair,*
> *And I will my bones to Joseph Flog, when they are picked quite bare.*
> *To Jack the Brush I will my tail, likewise my silken mare,*
> *To make a set of brushes to keep the people clane.*
> *And to the Irish piper I will my tender skin,*
> *'Twill make a fine new bellows for to supply the wind,*
> *To fill the streets with music at the pattern and the fair,*
> *To cheer the hearts of boys and girls dancing on Irish air.*[37]

It was indeed a strange world that has now gone.

# 8 Play

Perhaps that world was nowhere stranger than in its festivals, fairs, beliefs and amusements, and many of these to modern eyes seem strange and almost unbelievable. People no longer play games at wakes, and storytelling in the old style has almost come to an end. To describe life and tradition it is necessary to mention at least some of the elements which made life joyful in the midst of the poverty and sickness which occurred so often in the past.

As everywhere, children made their own amusements. The study of their games in rural Ireland is a neglected topic, yet the old games and pastimes were well recorded by the Folklore Commission in the 1930s. From even a cursory glance through these school notebooks it can be seen that children in many different areas had the same type of amusements. The national games of hurling and Gaelic football were very popular and almost every boy played; they were all avid supporters of the local teams, which usually represented the parish. Hurling is, of course, an ancient game reputedly played by some of the heroes of Irish mythology, while football is a more recent introduction though it was played in Kerry for centuries. Children also enjoyed the usual games of chasing, running and jumping. For smaller children nonsense rhymes were popular in all areas, and some of these in the Irish language such as 'Lurabóg: larabóg' were found in both Irish and English speaking districts. Other rhymes such as 'The big ship goes to the alli alli o' as well as being internationally known were also popular in Ireland. In recent years the growing popularity of children's books has tended to make international nursery rhymes better known in Ireland and many of the older rhymes are not often heard now. But as Eilís Brady has shown for Dublin, children retain traditional games far more than we realize.[1] It has often been noted by anthropologists that children's play is often imitative of their parents,[2] but in the modern world with the father away at work all day, it is usually only the mother that children can imitate. In rural Ireland in the past, however, where children grew up in close contact with both parents, their games often tended to be imitative of both parents' occupations. A beautiful toy boat excavated at High Street in Dublin

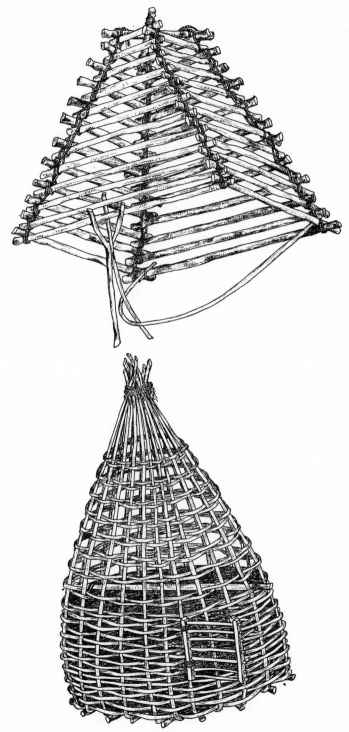

*Fig. 20. Thrushes' cage, Clonascra, Co. Offaly, and bird crib or trap, Kilcleagh, Co. Westmeath.*

shows that this was for long the case. Small girls made dolls with clothes similar
to those their mothers made for them; children made copies of the tools and
implements used by their fathers, and both children and adults made traps for
catching birds called cribs (fig. 20).

Cribs were the most common devices used for trapping, but a questionnaire
circulated by the National Museum in the 1960s showed that there was an enormous
variety of such items used in rural Ireland in the past. In Mucklagh, Co. Offaly,
bird lime was made from the bark of the holly tree and used to catch song-birds.
Cones of paper lined with lime and filled with corn were used to catch pheasants,
and on dark nights the same victims were caught by snares on the end of long
poles while dazzled by lights on their tree-branch roosts. Horsehair snares were
used for trout, and the list of such devices is as great as the countryman's ingenuity.
Small baskets made from green rushes were used for catching tiny fish and these
were known by a variety of names in different areas. In parts of Counties Offaly and
Wicklow they were known as 'pinkeen nets'[3] while in Roscommon and Galway
they were known as 'Leebeen boxes'. Similar cages made from green rushes were
used for butterflies in the midland counties. Throwing sticks were popular when
children went hunting, as were slings which in Co. Cork consisted of a 30-inch
long stick and a twine with two leather squares on it. A stone was placed in the
first leather patch, and the second, which was at the end of the twine, was held to
the side of the stick by the thumb; to release the stone when the sling was rotating
the thumb was lifted. But not all toys were as lethal and toy guns made out of
pieces of alder with the pith removed did no more than make a loud bang when a
spring mechanism was released. Toy ink was made from alder berries, and whistles
made from alder were also popular. In north Co. Dublin whistles were made
from pieces of ash 9 inches long and up to 1 inch in diameter. In making such
whistles the bark was removed in a single cylindrical piece and this later formed the
body of the whistle.[4] In the past rural Ireland was largely unaffected by the com-
mercialization of leisure which appears to have swept western Europe in the
eighteenth century. Children shared in the homely pleasures of the adult society
and relied, as did their elders, on the materials available locally to manufacture the
toys they required. The skill displayed in using such materials to manufacture
essential articles was also shown in their toys. This is seen at its best in charming
baby's rattles made from osiers or rushes with stones inside (fig. 21 and pl. 136).

Like other aspects of life and tradition in rural Ireland many games were of
great antiquity. Ireland's mythological heroes were adept at using a sling, and
buzzers, bull roarers, boards, papers or bones for making noise when spun, were
disapproved of in many areas as they were reputed to bring bad luck (pl. 134). It

*Fig. 21. Osier rattle, Ballinakilla, Co. Galway.*

has been suggested that these toys of today were connected with the pagan practices of an earlier period.[5] Gaming pieces have been discovered on many archaeological excavations and a particularly fine gaming board was found in a crannóg at Ballinderry. The late Eoin MacWhite in an article on early Irish board games showed that two of these, *fidchell* and *brandub* pre-date chess and draughts in Europe by at least five centuries on literary evidence alone, and that the Irish games were probably played in prehistoric times.[6] These games were forgotten about and are no longer played; indeed even the rules were never recorded. Dice were known in Ireland from at least the early historic period and by the seventeenth century cards and horse racing were popular in the anglicized areas.[7] It is certain that many of the new arrivals in Ireland through the centuries brought with them new games and that these spread to the native population, but it would, of course, be impossible to mention here all the sports and games of Ireland. Life in the towns in medieval Ireland was as elsewhere:

'Brimful of play: the joyous and unbuttoned play of the people, full of pagan elements that had lost their significance and had been transformed into jesting and baffoonery or the solemn and pompous play of chivalry, the sophisticated play of courtly love—In fine the influence of the play—spirit was extraordinarily great in the Middle Ages, not on the inward structure of its institutions, which was largely classical in origin, but on the ceremonial with which that structure was expressed and embellished.'[8]

In rural Ireland the play element was equally strong, and the mummers and the folk dramas performed in rural Ireland are probably a legacy of the medieval miracle plays mixed with the elements.[9] The hobby-horse, called in Munster the *Láir Bhán*, was an integral part of such plays (pl. 135). The significance of the horse is now forgotten, but this is one of the many customs, not confined to Ireland, whose origin and purpose are lost in the mist of antiquity. Rural Ireland preserved many of the older customs and traditions much longer than urban Ireland, where even the set pieces of civic ceremonials were dragged on as dull duties rather than opportunities for merriment in the eighteenth century.[10] In contrast, rural Ireland celebrated, and indeed in some places still celebrates, an enormous variety of festivals.

From the first of these, St Brighid's Day, 1st February, to Christmas, St Stephen's Day and Epiphany known in Ireland as 'Little Christmas' or *Nollaig na mBan* ('Women's Christmas') the calendar was full of regular festivals, some secular and others religious. The special food prepared for celebrations on such feast-days has already been mentioned, but food never appears to have been important, or perhaps it was never plentiful enough, for great orgies of eating to take place. Whiskey on the other hand, especially home-brewed, could be made easily from the ubiquitous potato. Poteen was always distilled in remote districts and in parts of north Donegal it was a peasant industry. From the number of reports of seizures of stills, worms, wash and equipment it is evident that the still remains a commercial enterprise in parts of the west[11] (pl. 139). Drink, it must be said, played an important part in many of the folk festivals and this possibly accounts for the unusually high proportion of our national income which is still spent on alcohol. Each festival had, however, its own significance and the form of the celebration was adapted accordingly. St Brighid's Day, 1st February, was not only the feast-day of the national female patron saint but also the beginning of the new agricultural year. In a less sophisticated society it marked the end of the privations of winter and the beginnings of growth and renewal. In pre-Christian times it was undoubtedly also a folk festival, and the early missionaries probably turned the old pagan feast into one of religious significance. St Brighid became the symbol of the season, and the year's agricultural prospects were regarded as depending on her intercession and consequently her feast-day was celebrated with due reverence. The omens observed on that day were carefully noted, but the ritual was of prime importance and this varied from district to district. The most common custom was that of making St Brighid's Crosses (pl. 137). These took different forms in different districts and were usually made either on the eve of the feast-day or on the day itself.[12] In the midlands only a small number of crosses were made, but in the north crosses were made in large numbers and placed in different places. In some areas a small folk play was enacted when a girl playing the part of the saint sought admission to the house, was allowed in, blessed the family, joined them for supper and helped make the crosses. In some areas a doll, sometimes made of straw and called a *Brideóg* represented the saint and was carried from house to house by a group in disguise who collected money or gifts. The rhymes used by the groups were handed down from generation to generation and probably are faint reminders of a medieval religious ceremony. The many aspects of the celebration of St Brighid's Day have been well described elsewhere,[13] and that day's celebration is typical of many other festive days in which religion, folk custom, and superstition concerning agriculture were closely associated. May Day was yet another folk festival which was closely connected with agriculture, and it was a day that represented the beginning of summer. In the high period of Irish landlordism it was also rent day. Folk custom dictated that may bushes should be decorated with ribbons, egg shells or flowers. In the midlands may pole dances were held and folk plays were performed in Wexford by mummers. The religious aspect of May Day was not great, though in that month many houses erected small altars with a statute and flowers in honour of Mary. Midsummer was always a time for celebration, though in some areas it was celebrated on the eve of St John's Day (23rd June) and in others on the eve of Sts Peter and Paul (28th June). Bonfires were built in many areas and in Co. Offaly this custom was still common on 28th June until the mid 1950s. The summer months were the hungry months during the long period of the country's dependence on the potato, and naturally the beginning of the harvesting of the new crop was celebrated. On the last Sunday in July the ancient festival of Lughnasa was celebrated and this marked the start of the harvesting. On that Sunday people travelled to the top of hills and there they held various kinds of celebrations. Visits to holy wells were common on all festive days. Lughnasa has now been turned into a religious festival in some areas and so thousands climb Croagh Patrick in Co. Mayo to pray on the spot where the national patron saint is reputed to have prayed. The end of the harvest was also celebrated in various ways,[14] and the cutting of the last sheaf was a complex folk festival of great antiquity in northern areas.[15] In Co. Offaly beautiful harvest knots were woven from straw and worn by both men and women (pl. 138). Halloween was the festival which marked the beginning of winter. In some areas, notably Galway, on St Martin's Eve (10th November) cocks were killed and blood sprinkled on the doors of houses. This was probably a survival from a period when animals were killed before the winter when fodder was difficult to obtain. It is yet another interesting example of the way in which religion and agriculture were mixed in Irish folk festivals.

There were also many other religious holidays. Of these Christmas and Easter were the most important and were widely celebrated. The form of the celebration at Easter shows that Easter was probably an old pagan festival, and the decoration of eggs, which was common in Ireland, is also recorded throughout Europe and even Asia. Lent was a period of abstinence dictated by church law, and its beginning was marked with a pancake party on Shrove Tuesday. The ban on marriage ceremonies for Catholics during Lent meant that unmarried Catholics remained in

*Fig. 22. Penal crucifix, Athboy, Co. Meath.*

that state until the following Easter at least and probably longer. In the past when people were encouraged to marry, this Lenten ban led to the custom on the first Sunday of Lent of marking the unmarried with chalk as they went to church—giving that day the name 'Chalk Sunday'. The custom was mainly one of fun, but rural society was never reluctant to show genuine disapproval and ageing,

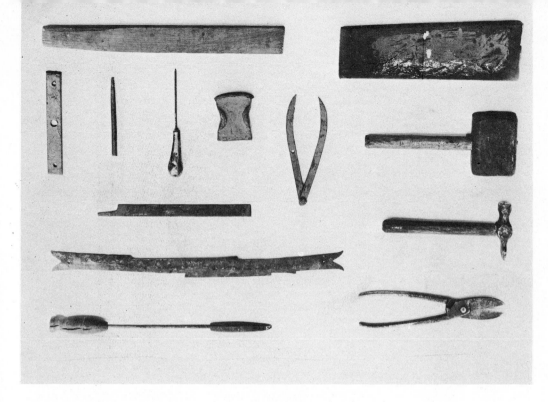

123. *Tinsmith's tools: clips, soldering iron, marking stick, hammer, file, mallet, compass, hand stake, awl, punch, nail tool, rosin board, scutcher* (N.M.I. GF133).

124. *Tinsmith's anvil and carrying case* (N.M.I. GF164).

*125. Roadside forge, Co. Donegal (B.F. TY31).*

*126. Banding wheels, Cloghane, Co. Kerry (B.F. 63/54).*

*127. Donegal weaver* (B.F. TY*35/53*).

*128. Scutching stock for flax, spinning wheel and clack wheel, Toome, Co. Antrim*
(*W. A. Green, 1017*).

129. Above left: *The village carpenter, Dunboyne, Co. Meath* (B.F. *47/53*).

130. Above right: *Wooden-framed flax breaker in disused mill at Ballynallon Bridge, Co. Cavan.*

131. *Pole lathe, Borrisokane, Co. Tipperary* (N.M.I. CF*445*).

*132. Pit sawing, Donard, Co. Wicklow* (N.M.I. DF36).

*133. Cooperage, Killarney, Co. Kerry* (N.L.I. 9985WL).

134. Bull roarer, Co. Carlow
(N.M.I. GF35).

136. Three rush rattles, Ballyfarnagh,
Co. Mayo, Ballinakill, Co. Galway,
and Armagh, Co. Armagh (N.M.I.
GF97).

135. Hobby-horse (láir bhán), Co. Kerry (N.M.I. EF50).

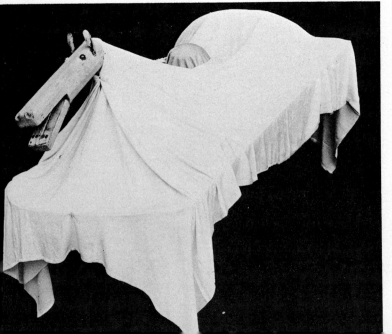

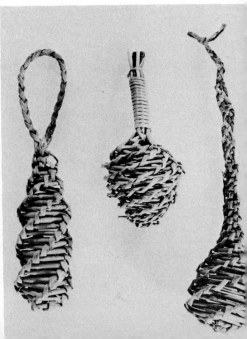

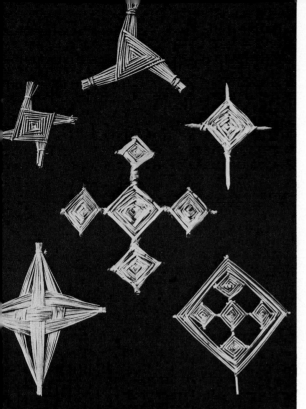

137. *St Brighid's Crosses.*

138. *Harvest knots (N.M.I. EF13).*

139. *Potheen still, Connemara (B.F. TY245).*

140. *Straw boy's costume. Suit, hide mask and hats from Counties Kerry and Mayo. Drawing by Miss E. Johnston (N.M.I. EF10).*

141. *Wren boy, Spiddal, Co. Galway.*

142. *Holy well, Doon, Co. Donegal (N.L.I. 3639WL).*

prosperous bachelors were teased maliciously. In recent years St Patrick's Day (17th March) has become the great national feast-day. Besides the usual religious feast-days there were in rural Ireland a great number of local saints whose feast-days were and are celebrated in the areas where they lived. Such days are called pattern days and can be confined to the people of a parish as is the case of St Carthage's Day in Rahan, Co. Offaly. At St Mullin's on the River Barrow people from Carlow, Kilkenny, Wexford and Waterford gather on a Sunday late in July to honour the miller saint at the site of the burial place of the MacMurrough Kavanaghs, the old kings of Leinster.[16] Every area had its own saint and great devotion to these created a special reason for celebrating their feast-days. Studies of the festivals are few though there are many short accounts. Kevin Danaher has compiled a fascinating account of calendar customs[17] and Máire Mac Neill's *The Festival of Lughnasa*[18] is a classical examination of one festival. This is an aspect of life in rural Ireland which deserves extensive examination, especially now as the older folk festivals are disappearing and a myriad variety of new festivals aimed at promoting tourism are beginning. Some of these incorporate the older folk festivals and this tendency is to be welcomed.

The principal forms of entertainment for people in rural Ireland in the past were storytelling, music, dancing and song. In Ireland the social setting within which folklore and indeed folk custom flourished was still to be found until this century. This means that there was an unbroken line of tradition of such story-telling back to earliest historical times. Stories were told by the fireside during the long winter nights, and sessions usually began with the man of the house telling the first tale. He was followed by neighbours and if a travelling craftsman, labourer or beggar was in the company the opportunity of hearing a new story or a new variation of a well-known story was greatly appreciated. A good storyteller was greatly honoured and a traveller with this talent was always assured of a hearty welcome. The art of storytelling still survives, but is now confined to a very small band who usually only practise their art for the sake of having their stories recorded. The social settings have changed and it is impossible for the narrator to compete with the excitement, colour and sound of the television set on the other side of the room. Many of the stories told until recently were of great antiquity and of international appeal. The oldest stories were those of the Ulster cycle with their heroes Cochobhar, Cuchulainn and his son, Déirdre and the sons of Uisneach; these tales have been ascribed a date in the early years of the Christian period. The more popular Fenian cycle are of slightly later composition and have Fíonn Mac Cumhail as the principal hero. Besides these two main cycles of stories there are numerous other traditional stories which have kings as heroes while in others saints, poets, youths or craftsmen are the principal characters. Many stories can be dated to the medieval period, especially those with a religious character or themes; other stories told at rustic firesides were also known in other lands. Seán Ó Súilleabháin and R. Th. Christiansen's catalogue of Irish tales shows that at least 43,000 versions of 700 international tale types have been recorded in Ireland.[19] These include animal tales, folk tales, jokes, anecdotes, hero stories and formula tales.

Storytelling was, of course, originally in the Irish language and for particular types of folklore the Irish-speaking districts produced the richest material. The rich folklore of Ireland was not confined to these areas and even in Leinster recordings show that the same tradition survived the transition from Gaelic to English. This golden treasure of the humble countryman survived through the centuries, as indeed did the folk music and dance of the people. In the houses of the country people storytelling, music and dancing brought gaiety to people whose lives were often deprived of many material comforts. It was these aspects of life and tradition that made so many Irish emigrants remember their homeland with such fond affection. Significantly some of the finest early collections of Irish music were made by emigrants in America from their companions.[20]

There is of course a strong connection between all aspects of folk custom. Song and dance played an important part in the celebrations of the festive days in Ireland. Wren dances held on St Stephen's Night were made more enjoyable as many of those attending spent the day going from house to house collecting money to bury the wren (pl. 141); the money was usually used to buy drink or food to aid the night's festivities. Usually everybody in a community was involved. For the children the donning of strange costumes in the morning began the enjoyment and even the oldest could enjoy the singing, dancing and storytelling at the wren dance which could continue well into the night. Ritual rhymes, song, dance, storytelling and folk custom combined to make these festive days truly enjoyable. The custom of dressing up in straw costume to escort the bride to a wedding in Sligo is a joyful aspect of this tradition (pl. 140).[21] In the south-west the blowing of outlandish noises on cow's horns around the honeymoon house as a sign of disapproval of the marriage is yet another aspect of this tradition. The ritual faction fighting is difficult to understand in modern society, while games played at wakes appear equally barbaric. To understand the life style of people in the past it is necessary to try and recreate all aspects of their lives, but folk custom cannot be adequately described in these few pages. The food, houses, furniture, dress, employment and entertainments of a people must be seen as influences combining to create an overall life style.

It was stated above that many traditional tales were found in Leinster in the English language. The Cinderella story is well known in many lands and many versions have been recorded. A version found in Carlow and west Wicklow gives the flavour of the story as told in the dialect of that district. When it is remembered that this story was heard and enjoyed in the log cabins of northern Sweden, in Germany and in other lands it can be seen that this is truly an aspect of European culture that is worthy of attention:

'Once upon a time there was a king and queen, and they had three daughters. There was two of them lovely girls, and Hairy Rucky. Hairy Rucky was always in the corner. And this old king and the queen they got poor, and the two daughters went off to seek their fortune. So Hairy Rucky said she'd go too, and she started after them, and the two daughters waited for her to see what they would do. So they tied her to a tree. When they got up a good way again they looked back, and here was Hairy Rucky coming with the tree on her back! So when she came on again they saw a stack of hay, and they put a chain all round it, and tied her to it, and then they went on, and when they were a long ways off they looked back, and here was Hairy Rucky coming with the tree and rick of hay on her back! So they shoved her into a clamp of turf, and dressed her up in it, and when they went on here she come with the clamp of turf on her back!

'So the two of them came to a king's place, and the king hired the two of them, and Hairy Rucky came up and the king hired her also.

'The king had three daughters of his own, and he sent for his wife and he said: "Make a bed for these three daughters". The two daughters didn't want to let Hairy Rucky sleep with them at all. So she had to sleep somewhere else, but she kept always knocking about somewhere outside.

'She was sort of enchanted, and she knew everything that was going on. The king wanted to cut the heads off of Hairy Rucky's two sisters that night. So what did Hairy Rucky do only go up and take the king's two daughters out of their bed, and put them into her sisters' bed, and her own two sisters back into the king's bed. So, begor, when the king went up he killed his own two daughters.

'The next morning when he had seen what he had done he went mad, and said he would do away with the two girls; and Hairy Rucky went in and she done away with the old king.

'So the three of them took any money there was around the place, and they went home, and they were living comfortable with all the money they had.

'Hairy Rucky couldn't be got out of the ashes. So there was a great ball coming off, and the two daughters were invited to go to the ball, because they had plenty of money and gold, and everything, the way they could go anywhere to this king's house; and Hairy Rucky said she'd go too. So they wouldn't let her go. So the two started off to the ball, and during the time they were gone a witch came into Hairy Rucky; and there was six mice in the trap and a rat, and she turned the mice into six horses and the rat into a coachman, and touched Hairy Rucky with her wand, and she was a lovely girl. She bid Hairy Rucky go on to the spree: "Only stop till nine o'clock. Don't stop a minute after nine o'clock, because if you do you won't have any coach or any horses to drive you home . You'll be a Hairy Rucky again".

'So at nine o'clock she was to come home; but that night she fell in love with the king's son; and dancing and everything. But when it come nine o'clock says she: "I have to go". And he thought to hold her, but she got away, and the coach was yoked outside the door for her. So she got home before the girls, and when the girls come home she asked them what sort of a time they had, and they were telling her about the grand girl came there in the coach. Hairy Rucky said nothing.

'So they had to go the next night again. So the two wouldn't let her go. She pressed hard to go but they wouldn't let her go. But the witch come on again, and she got the coachman and the horses and all for her, and had her lovelier than the night before. So she could stop till half nine this night, but not a minute later. So she went on, and the king's son met her when she went into the yard with the coach and brought her on to where they put up the horses; but at half nine she made for the door, and she got out to the coach and got home, and the two sisters came home, and said there was a lovelier girl there that night.

'The third night the two daughters had to go, and Hairy Rucky got a nicer coach; and all better dressed and started off, and she got till ten o'clock and not a minute later. She heard ten striking, and she made for the door, and the coach was waiting in the yard, and she lost one of her slippers. So she got up in the coach and drove home. But the row took place about who owned the slipper anyway, because the king's son wouldn't wed anyone except the one that owned the glass shoe. So they started out to search through the country everywhere, and they could find no girl that the slipper would fit. They came to Hairy Rucky's; and the two daughters was shaving their feet trying to get the slipper on, but it wouldn't fit them; and they asked was there another girl there, and they said there was. So they brought her down anyway, and the very minute they did the slipper run in on her foot, and she peeled off the old clothes and she had a clean skin inside. So Hairy Rucky got married to the king's son.

'*So put down the kettle and make tay*
*And if they don't live happy, that I may.*'[22]

# Notes

1 HOUSES

1 A. Gailey, 'The thatched houses of Ulster' in *Ulster Folklife*, 7, 1961, p. 12.

2 C. Ó'Danachair, 'Irish vernacular architecture in relation to the Irish Sea' in *The Irish Sea Province* (Cambrian Archaeological Association, 1970), p. 98.

3 *Ordnance Survey Letters, Westmeath* (1837), pp. 28–9; *Ormonde Deeds*, III (1338), p. 375; P. Harbison, *Guide to National Monuments of Ireland* (Dublin, 1970), p. 26.

4 S. P. Ó'Ríordáin, 'Excavations at Cush, Co. Limerick' in *Proceedings of The Royal Irish Academy*, XLV, C, pp. 83–181; S. P. Ó'Ríordáin and M. J. O'Kelly, 'Old house types near Lough Gur, Co. Limerick' in *Feil— Sgribhinn Eoin Mhic Neill*, 1940, pp. 227–36.

5 Throughout this book different ages are mentioned; the following table gives a rough guide to the dates of the various ages:

Mesolithic   7000–4000 BC
Neolithic   4000–2000 BC
Bronze   2000–500 BC
Iron   500 BC–AD 500.
Early Christian   AD 500–1169.
Medieval   AD 1169–1540.

6 S. P. Ó'Ríordáin, op. cit.

7 S. P. Ó'Ríordáin, *Antiquities of the Irish countryside* (London, 1974), p. 1.

8 V. B. Proudfoot, 'The economy of the Irish rath' in *Medieval Archaeology*, 5, 1961.

9 C. Ó'Danachair, 'Representations of houses on some Irish maps of c. 1600' in *Studies in folk life* (London, 1969), pp. 91–104.

10 E. E. Evans, *Prehistoric Ireland and Early Christian Ireland* (London, 1866), p. 96.

11 W. G. Wood Martin, *Lake dwellings of Ireland* (Dublin, 1886), p. 26.

12 H. O'Neill Hencken, 'Ballinderry crannóg, No. 1' in *Proceedings of the Royal Irish Academy*, 43, 1934–6, pp. 103–226, 120.

13 R. Buchanan, 'Rural settlement in Ireland' in *Irish geographical studies* (Belfast, 1970), p. 149.

14 D. Ó'Corráin, *Ireland before the Normans* (Dublin, 1972), p. 61.

15 A. T. Lucas, 'The plundering and burning of churches in Ireland, 7th to 16th century' in *North Munster studies* (Limerick, 1967), p. 172–229.

16 H. G. Leask, *Irish castles and castellated houses* (Dundalk, 1944), pp. 75–92.

17 S. P. Ó'Ríordáin and J. Hunt, 'Medieval dwellings at Caherguillamore, Co. Limerick' in *Journal of the Royal Society of Antiquaries of Ireland*, 72, 1942, pp. 37–63.

18   D. McCourt, 'The dynamic quality of Irish rural settlement' in *Man and his habitat* (London 1971), p. 152.

19   Ibid., pp. 152–60.

20   R. H. Buchanan, 'Field systems of Ireland' in A. R. H. Baker and R. A. Butlin (eds.), *Studies in field systems in the British isles* (Cambridge, 1973), pp. 609–13; R. E. Glasscock, 'Moated sites and deserted boroughs and village: two neglected aspects of Anglo-Norman settlement in Ireland' in *Irish geographical studies* (Belfast, 1970), pp. 162–77.

21   M. Drake, 'The Irish demographic crises of 1740–41' in Irish Historical Studies, vi, ed. T. W. Moody, (London 1968), p. 121.

22   K. H. Connell, *The population of Ireland* (Oxford, 1950), pp. 1–26.

23   Census of Ireland, 1841, H.C. 1843 (503), XXIV.

24   T. P. O'Neill, 'Poverty in Ireland, 1815–45' in *Folk Life*, XI, 1973, pp. 28–9.

25   C. Ó'Danachair, 'The bothán scóir' in *North Munster studies* (Limerick, 1967), p. 489–98; T. P. O'Neill, 'Clare and Irish poverty, 1815–1851' in *Studia Hibernica*, 14, 1974, pp. 7–27.

26   C. Ó'Danachair, op. cit., 1970, fig. 24.

27   S. Erixon, 'West European connections and cultural relations' in *Folkliv*, 2, 1938, p. 170.

28   A. T. Lucas, 'Contributions to the history of the Irish house: a possible ancestry of the bed-outshot' in *Folk Life*, 8, 1970, pp. 81–98.

29   D. McCourt, 'The outshot house-type and its distribution in Co. Londonderry' in *Ulster Folklife*, 2, 1956, pp. 27–34.

30   C. Ó'Danachair, 'The combined byre-and-dwelling in Ireland' in *Folk Life*, 2, 1964, pp. 58–75.

31   D. McCourt, 'The house and bedroom over byre' in *Ulster Folklife*, 15/16, 1970, pp. 3–19.

32   A Gailey, 'Rural housing in mid-nineteenth-century Ulster' in *Rural housing in Ulster in the mid nineteenth century* (H.M.S.O., n.d.), p. 6.

33   C. Ó'Danachair, 'Irish vernacular architecture in relation to the Irish sea' in *The Irish Sea Province* (Cambrian Archaeological Association, 1970, pp. 98–107.

34   D. McCourt, 'Innovation diffusion in Ireland: an historical case study' in *Proceedings of the Royal Irish Academy*, 73, C, 1, 1973, p. 14.

35   Ibid., pp. 18–19.

36   C. Ó'Danachair, op. cit., 1970, pp. 98–100.

37   D. McCourt, 'Roof timbering techniques in Ulster' in *Folk Life*, 10, 1972, pp. 118–30.

38   C. Ó'Danachair, 'Some distributional patterns in Irish folk life' in *Béaloideas*, 25, 1957, pp. 108–23.

39   I. F. Grant, *Highland folk ways* (London, 1961), p. 144.

40   *Poor Report*, 1836 (37), XXXII, appendix E, p. 58.

41   A. Gailey, 'Rural housing in mid-nineteenth century Ulster' in *Rural housing in Ulster in the mid nineteenth century* (H.M.S.O., n.d.), pp. 7–8.

42   Michael Mac Énrí, letter 2.12.1294 (N.M.I.).

43   See for example P. Kennedy, *Fireside stories of Ireland* (Dublin, 1870), or D. Hyde, *Beside the fire* (Dublin, 1890).

44   *Rural housing in Ulster in the mid nineteenth century* (H.M.S.O., n.d.), p. D; E. E. Evans, 'Sod and turf houses in Ireland' in *Studies in folk life* (London, 1969), 79–90.

45   C. Ó'Danachair, 'Materials and methods in Irish traditional building'

in *Journal of the Royal Society of Antiquaries of Ireland*, 87, 1957, pp. 61–74.

46 E. E. Evans, *Irish folk ways* (London, 1957), p. 49; J. Hall, *Tour of Ireland* (London, 1813), I, p. 277.

47 A. T. Lucas, 'Wattle and straw mat doors in Ireland' in *Artica* (Uppsala, 1956), pp. 16–35.

48 A. T. Lucas, 'A straw roof lining at Stradbally, Co. Waterford' in *Journal of the Royal Society of Antiquaries of Ireland*, 76, 1971, pp. 81–3.

49 E. E. Evans and D. McCourt, 'Farmhouse at Shantallow' in *Ulster Folklife*, 14, 1968, pp. 20–1.

50 I.F.C., MS. Vol. 65, p. 195, Vol. 407, p. 266, Vol. 389, pp. 254–6.

51 S. Ó'Súilleabháin, 'Foundation sacrifices' in *Journal of the Royal Society of Antiquaries of Ireland*, 75, 1945, pp. 45–52.

52 D. Hyde, *Saints and sinners* (Dublin, 1915), pp. 202–5.

53 *Béaloideas*, VII, 169.

54 P. Danaher, 'A prehistoric burial mound at Ballyesaken, Co. Sligo' in *Journal of the Royal Society of Antiquaries of Ireland*, 94, 1964, pp. 145–56.

55 A. Gailey, 'The thatched houses of Ulster' in *Ulster Folklife*, 7, 1961, pp. 16–17.

56 Hammond Innes, *Sea and islands* (London, 1967), p. 235.

## 2 FURNITURE

1 J. C. O'Sullivan, 'St. Brigid's Crosses' in *Folk Life*, XI, 1973; T. G. F. Patterson, *Harvest Home* (Dundalk, 1975), pp. 193–7 (E. E. Evans, ed.).

2 A. Gailey, 'Kitchen furniture' in *Ulster Folklife*, 12, 1966, pp. 18–34.

3 A. Gailey, op. cit., pp. 28–9.

4 *Dunton Letters*, 448–24.

5 Quoted in C. Otway, *Sketches in Erris and Tyrawly* (Dublin, 1850), p. 48.

6 I.F.C., MS. Vol. 141, p. 1080.

7 C. Otway, op. cit., p. 32.

8 J. C. Walker, *Historical memoirs of the Irish bards* (Dublin, 1918), appendix 1, pp. 196–204; *Béaloideas*, IX, p. 294.

9 J. McParlan, *Statistical survey of Co. Mayo* (Dublin, 1802), p. 65; see also P. Knight, *Erris and the Atlantic railway* (Dublin, 1836), p. 177.

10 E. E. Evans, *Irish folk ways* (London, 1957), p. 87.

11 Rev. G. Hill, *An historical account of the Plantation of Ulster* (Belfast, 1877), p. 244.

12 C. Otway, op. cit., p. 28.

13 A. Gailey, op. cit. pp. 25–9.

14 I.F.C., MS. Vol. 107. p. 44.

15 *Béaloideas*, XIV, p. 60.

16 See examples in folk life collections of National Museum of Ireland.

17 J. Hall, *Tour through Ireland* (London, 1813), I, p. 277.

18 I.F.C., MS. Vol. 44, pp. 407–8.

19 *Béaloideas*, VI, p. 265.

20 I.F.C., MS. Vol. 259, p. 652.

21 *Béaloideas*, XIV, p. 105.

22 Ibid., XIII, p. 138.

23 Ibid., X, pp. 286–7.

24 I.F.C., MS. Vol. 117, p. 96.

25 G. T. Stokes (ed.), *Pococke's tour in Ireland, 1752* (Dublin, 1891), p. 87.

26 J. Hall, *Tour through Ireland* (London, 1813), I, p. 277.

27 G. Jenkins, *Traditional country crafts-men* (London, 1965), p. 142.

28 P. Kennedy, *Legendary fictions of the Irish Celts* (London, 1866), p. 100.

29 Kevin Danaher, *The pleasant land of Ireland* (Cork 1970), p. 49.

30 S. M. Tibbott, 'Sucan and Ilymru in Wales' in *Folk Life*, 12, 1974, p. 31.

31   *Béaloideas*, IX, p. 293.

32   S. Erixon, 'West European connections and cutural relations' in *Folkliv*, 2, 1938, pp. 137–72.

33   A. Gailey, op. cit., p. 18.

34   'The Dublin shopkeeper's address to the gentlemen White Boys' in *Cork Hibernian Chronicle*, 2 March 1786, p. 1 (the Dublin shopkeeper was John B. Bennett).

35   G. T. Stokes (ed.), op. cit., p. 87.

36   J. Small (ed.), *The image of Ireland by John Derriche, 1581* (Edinburgh, 1883), p. 54.

37   A. T. Lucas, 'Washing and bathing in ancient Ireland' in *Journal of the Royal Society of Antiquaries of Ireland*, 95, 165, p. 83.

38   M. F. Ryan, 'Native pottery in early historic Ireland' in *Proceedings of the Royal Irish Academy*, C, 73, 11, pp. 630–3.

39   P. F. Wallace, 'Medieval skillets in the National Museum of Ireland', forthcoming.

40   Ibid. See also E. McCracken, *Irish woods since Tudor times* (Belfast, 1971), pp. 90–6 and 165–8.

41   S. P. Ó'Ríordáin, *Antiquities of the Irish countryside* (London, 1974), pp. 43–5.

42   A. T. Lucas, 'Washing and bathing in ancient Ireland' in *Journal of the Royal Society of Antiquaries of Ireland*, 95, 1965, p. 80.

43   H. F. Berry (ed.), *Register of wills and inventories of the diocese of Dublin . . . 1457–83* (Dublin, 1896–7).

44   G. T. Stokes (ed.), op. cit., p. 87; C. Otway, op. cit., p. 29.

45   See below, p. 40.

46   *Irish delftware: a Rosc exhibition catalogue* (Dublin, 1971).

47   K. Danaher, *The pleasant land of Ireland* (Cork, 1970), pp. 62 and 65.

48   S. Gmelch and P. Langan, *Tinkers and travellers* (Dublin, 1975), p. 28.

49   Ibid., pp. 8–44.

50   K. Danaher, *In Ireland long ago* (Cork, 1969), pp. 31–2.

51   Pococke in 1752 wrote of Co. Mayo: 'All their vessels are of wood, most of them cut out of solid timber, their stools are long and narrow like a stilion, and their table is a long sort of stool about 20 inches high and broad and two yards long', G. T. Stokes (ed.), op. cit., p. 87.

52   A. Gailey, op. cit., pp. 23–5.

53   P. Kennedy, *Evenings in Duffrey* (Dublin, 1875), pp. 38 and 66; also records in I.F.C.

54   The tradition of scrubbing or scouring tables goes back to the 1830s, C. Otway, op. cit., p. 29.

55   Appendix E to 1835 *Poor Report, Parliamentary Papers*, 1836 (37), XXXII, pp. 69 and 90.

56   C. Ó'Síocháin, *The man from Cape Clear* (Cork, 1975), p. 80 (R. P. Breathnach's translation).

57   Ibid., p. 3.

58   E. E. Evans, *Irish folk ways* (London, 1972), pp. 89–92.

59   G. T. Stokes (ed.) op. cit., p. 87.

60   K. Danaher, *The pleasant land of Ireland* (Cork, 1970), p. 49.

61   H. F. Berry, op. cit., p. 102.

62   Ibid., p. 129.

63   R. Dunlop, 'The plantation of Leix and Offaly' in *English Historical Review*, VI, 1891, p. 189.

64   Rev. G. Hill, op. cit., p. 244.

65   T. P. O'Neill, 'Poverty in Ireland, 1815–45' in *Folk Life*, XI, 1973, pp. 22–33; A. T. Lucas, 'Irish folk life' in *British Association for the Advancement of Science* (Dublin, 1957), pp. 196–7.

## 3 THE DAY'S WORK

1 S. P. Ó'Ríordáin, *Antiquities of the Irish countryside* (London, 1942), pp. 43–6.

2 M. L. Ryder, 'Can one cook in a skin?' in *Antiquity*, Vol. 40, 1966, pp. 225–7; see also M. L. Ryder in *Antiquity*, Vol. 48, 1969, pp. 218–28.

3 Rev. G. Hill, *An historical account of the plantation of Ulster* (Belfast, 1877), pp. 224–6; B. Rich, *A new description of Ireland* (London, 1610), p. 39.

4 E. E. Evans, *Irish folk ways* (London, 1957), pp. 95–7.

5 Ibid., p. 96.

6 K. Danaher, *In Ireland long ago* (Cork, 1962), pp. 97–103.

7 W. O'Sullivan, *The economic history of Cork city* (Dublin, 1937); J. S. Donnelly, 'Cork market; its role in the nineteenth century Irish butter trade' in *Studia Hibernica*, 11, 1971, pp. 130–63.

8 J. Derricke, *The image of Ireland* (London, 1581), p. 374.

9 A. T. Lucas, 'Making wooden sieves' in *Journal of the Royal Society of Antiquaries of Ireland*, 81, 1951, pp. 146–55.

10 A. T. Lucas, 'The horizontal mill in Ireland' in *Journal of the Royal Society of Antiquaries of Ireland*, 83, 1953, pp. 1–36.

11 A. Fenton, *Scottish country life* (Edinburgh, 1976), pp. 101–2.

12 Information recorded from Mrs Anne Geraghty by Ciarán Bairéad, B.A., Dept. of Folklore, U.C.D.

13 A. Gailey, 'Ropes and rope twisters' in *Ulster Folklife*, 8, 1962, pp. 72–82.

14 K. Danaher, *The pleasant land of Ireland* (Cork, 1970), pp. 67–9.

15 P. Logan, *Making the cure* (Dublin, 1974).

16 M. J. Murphy, *At Slieve Gullion's foot* (Dundalk, 1941), p. 11.

17 J. P. Joly, *Diary*, Oct. 1846–May 1847 (N.L.I., MS. 17,035).

## 4 COSTUME

1 H. F. McClintock, *Old Irish and Highland dress* (Dundalk, 1950), pp. 125–7.

2 T. P. O'Neill, 'Eamonn Ceannt' in *Wine and gold* (Dublin, 1966), pp. 25–26.

3 L. P. Curtis, *Apes and angles, the Irishman in Victorian caricature* (Newtown Abbot, 1971).

4 F. G. Paine, 'Welsh peasant costume' in *Folk Life*, II, 1964, pp. 42–57.

5 J. C. Walker, *An historical essay on the dress of the ancient and modern Irish* (Dublin, 1818), Vol. II, pp. 1–2.

6 A. S. Henshall, 'Textiles and weaving appliances in prehistoric Britain' in *Proceedings of the Prehistoric Society*, 10, 1950, pp. 130–62.

7 H. F. McClintock, op. cit., pp. 25–26.

8 W. K. Sullivan's introduction to E. O'Curry, *On the manners and customs of the ancient Irish* (London, 1873), pp. ccclxxviii–ccccvii.

9 J. C. Walker, op. cit., pp. 25–6.

10 W. K. Sullivan, op. cit., pp. cccc–ccccvi; see also manuscript accounts in National Museum of dyes used until recently in rural Ireland.

11 A. T. Lucas, 'Footwear in Ireland' in *Co. Louth Archaeological Journal*, vol. 13, 4, 1956, pp. 340–94.

12 Quoted in H. F. McClintock, op. cit., p. 20.

13 J. C. Walker, op. cit. p. 88; L. M. Cullen, *Life in Ireland* (London, 1968), pp. 47–8.

14 Quoted in H. F. McClintock, op. cit., p. 74.

15 Quoted in J. C. Walker, op. cit., p. 86.

16 Men's clothes in the old fashion were still worn. See A. S. Henshall and W. A. Selby, 'The Dungiven costume' in *Ulster Journal of Archaeology*, vols. 24–5, 1961–2, pp. 119–42.

17 'National Museum Acquisitions, 1969' in *Journal of the Royal Society of Antiquaries*, vol. 102, 2, 1972, pp. 215–22. Description based on Miss Rosaline Murphy's observations.

18 T. P. O'Neill, 'Poverty in Ireland, 1815–45' in *Folk Life*, XI, 1973, p. 31.

19 Quoted in H. F. McClintock, op. cit., pp. 113–15.

20 T. C. Croker, *Researches in the south of Ireland* (London, 1824), quoted in L. Jones, 'The myth of Irish national costume' in *Ulster Transport and Folk Museum Annual Report*, 1971–2.

21 A. T. Lucas, 'The hooded cloak in Ireland in the nineteenth century' in *Journal of the Cork Historical and Archaeological Society*, vol. lvi, 1951, pp. 104–19.

22 J. Barrow, *A tour round Ireland* (London, 1836), p. 261.

23 A. K. Longfield, *Catalogue of the collection of lace in the National Museum of Ireland* (Dublin, n.d.).

24 A. T. Lucas, 'Some traditional methods of cloth finishing' in *The Advancement of Science*, 24, 120, Dec. 1967, pp. 184–92; A. T. Lucas, 'Cloth finishing in Ireland' in *Folk Life*, 6, 1968, pp. 18–67.

25 L. Mitchell, 'Looking for Irish traditional spinners' in *Quarterly Journal of the Association of Guilds of Weavers, Spinners and Dyers*, no. 90, 1974, pp. 1839–40.

26 The following eighteenth-century account from the Rosses in Donegal illustrates this:

'When the weather was favourable, the women frequently assembled in some neighbouring field, convenient to their huts, where they amused themselves with knitting and singing in the sun. The oldest, forming a circular group, sat working in the middle; round them the rest in circles, according to their years; the younger surrounding those of greater age, and singing alternate, and some-times in chorus, while the elder continued knitting. Their songs, called *speic-seoachs*, were recitals of exploits achieved by the giants, warriors and hunters of old.'

Rev. A. B., 'An account of the customs, manners and dress of the inhabitants of the Rosses' in J. C. Walker, op. cit., vol. 2, p. 202. A hundred years later spinning parties were common around Westport, Co. Mayo: H. Coulter, *The west of Ireland* (London, 1862), pp. 189–90 and illustration opposite p. 189; Patrick Gallagher, *The cottage crafts of our mountain women* (typescript memoirs, Dublin, 1972).

27 T. P. O'Neill, 'Fever and public health in pre-famine Ireland' in *Journal of the Royal Society of Antiquaries of Ireland*, 1973, 1, 175, pp. 1–38.

28 E. Keive, *The sacred history of knitting* (Oxford, 1971), pp. 65–70.

5 FOOD

1 A. T. Lucas, 'Cattle in ancient and medieval Irish society' in *O'Connell School Union Record, 1937–1958*, p. 1.

2 Ibid., p. 4.

3   Rev. R. H. Murray (ed.), *The journal of John Stevens* (Oxford, 1912), p. 139.

4   Kuno Meyer (ed.), *The vision of MacConglinne* (London, 1892), *passim*.

5   A. T. Lucas, 'Irish food before the potato' in *Gwerin*, III, 2, 1960, pp. 12–24; M. Ó Sé, 'Old Irish cheeses' in *Journal of the Cork Historical and Archaeological Society*, 53, 1948, pp. 82–97.

6   A. T. Lucas, 'Souterrains: the literary evidence' in *Béaloideas*, 39–41, 1971–73, pp. 165–91.

7   Kuno Meyer (ed.), op. cit., p. xxxiv.

8   A. T. Lucas, 'The horizontal mill in Ireland' in *Journal of the Royal Society of Antiquaries of Ireland*, 83, 1953, pp. 1–36.

9   A. Gailey, 'Irish corn drying kilns' in *Studies in folklife presented to E. E. Evans* (Belfast, 1970), pp. 64–9.

10  A. T. Lucas, 'Irish food before the potato' in *Gwerin*, III, 2, 1960 p. 2.

11  C. O'Donachair, 'Bread' in *Ulster Folklife*, 4, 1958, p. 29.

12  J. Derricke, *The image of Ireland* (1581), p. 374; A. T. Lucas, 'Irish food before the potato' in *Gwerin*, III, 2, 1960 pp. 8–10.

13  Kuno Meyer (ed.), op. cit., p. 36; see also p. 66.

14  See for example A. E. J. Went, 'An ancient fish weir at Ballyvartray, Co. Waterford, Ireland' in *Antiquity*, 25, 1951, pp. 32–5, and other articles by the same author; C. Ó'Síocháin, *The man from Cape Clear*, pp. 25–33, 153–4 (R. P. Breathnach's translation).

15  K. Danaher, *In Ireland long ago* (Cork, 1969), p. 54.

16  K. H. Connell, 'Illicit distillation: an Irish peasant industry' in *Historical Studies*, 3, 1961, pp. 58–91.

17  W. D. Davidson, 'The history of the potato and its progress in Ireland' in *Journal of the Department of Agriculture*, XXXIV, 1937, pp. 286–7.

18  R. N. Salaman, *The history and social influence of the potato* (Cambridge, 1949).

19  L. M. Cullen, 'Irish history without the potato' in *Past and Present*, 40, pp. 72–83.

20  A. Young, *Tour in Ireland, 1776–9* (London, 1892).

21  K. Danaher, *The year in Ireland* (Cork, 1972), pp. 163–6.

22  T. P. O'Neill, 'Clare and Irish poverty 1815–45' in *Studia Hibernica*, 12, 1974, pp. 7–27.

23  K. H. Connell, op. cit., pp. 147–51.

24  P. M. A. Bourke, 'The use of the potato crop in pre-famine Ireland', paper read before the Statistical and Social Inquiry Society of Ireland, 1 March 1968, pp. 9 and 16.

25  T. P. O'Neill, 'Poverty in Ireland, 1815–45' in *Folk Life*, II, 1973, p. 30.

26  A. MacLochlainn, 'Social life in County Clare, 1800–1850' in *University Review*, II, 1, Spring 1972, p. 63.

27  A. T. Lucas, 'Nettles and charlock as famine foods' in *Journal of the Breifne Historical Society*, I, 2, pp. 137–46.

27a *Rural housing in Ulster in the mid-nineteenth century* (Belfast, n.d.).

28  J. Derricke, op. cit., p. 376.

29  T. P. O'Neill, 'Poverty in Ireland, 1815–45' in *Folk Life*, II, 1973, p. 22.

30  Nils-Arvid Bringeus, 'Man, food and milieu' in *Folk Life*, 8, 1970, pp. 45–56.

31  T. P. O'Neill, 'The Catholic Church and the relief of the poor, 1815–45' in *Archivium Hibernicum*, XXXI, 1974, pp. 132–45.

32  Department of Irish Folklore, U.C.D., MS. 66, p. 155.

33  Nils-Arvid Bringeus, op. cit., p. 55.

34  A. T. Lucas, 'Irish food before the potato' in *Gwerin*, III, 2, 1960, p. 11.

35 T. P. O'Neill, 'Fever and public health in pre-famine Ireland' in *Journal of the Royal Society of Antiquaries of Ireland*, 103, I, 1975, pp. 1–38.

36 K. Danaher, *The year in Ireland* (Cork, 1972), pp. 54–7.

37 *Béaloideas*, XI, pp. 194–5.

38 I.F.C., MS. 407, p. 136.

39 R. H. Murray (ed.), op. cit, p. 139.

40 W. Carleton, *Dennis O'Shaughnessy going to Maynooth* (London, 1845), pp. 125–6.

41 F. O'Connor, *Leinster, Munster and Connaught* (London, n.d.), pp. 183–4.

42 *Cork Constitution*, 11th August 1886.

43 The name given to this cake was *multachán*, I.F.C., MS. 147, p. 169.

44 J. D. O'Dowd, 'Prerequisite of hereditary smiths' in *Béaloideas*, X, 1940, p. 287.

45 K. Danaher, *In Ireland long ago* (Cork, 1969), p. 39.

46 I.F.C., MS. 407, p. 29.

47 T. Fitzgibbon, *A taste of Ireland* (London, 1968), p. 91.

48 S. MacGiollarnáth, *Annála Beaga* (Dublin, 1941), pp. 271–2.

49 K. Danaher, *The year in Ireland* (Cork, 1972), p. 259.

50 I.F.C., MS. 39, p. 47.

51 C. Ó'Siocháin, op. cit., p. 3.

52 T. G. F. Patterson, 'County Armagh apples' in E. E. Evans (ed.), *Harvest home, the last sheaf* (Dundalk, 1975), p. 88.

53 E. E. Evans, *Irish folkways* (London, 1957), p. 73.

54 Ibid., p. 44.

55 K. Danaher, *The year in Ireland* (Cork, 1972), pp. 79–81.

56 P. Ó'Moghráin, 'The cake dance' in *Béaloideas*, 15, 1945, pp. 272–4.

57 *Irish Times*, 20th December 1967.

58 Rev. A. B., 'An account of the customs, manners and dress of the inhabitants of the Rosses' in J. C. Walker, *An historical essay on the dress of the ancient and modern Irish* (Dublin, 1818), pp. 201–2.

59 T. Fitzgibbon, op. cit., p. 61 and 103.

60 D. Bennett, *Irish Georgian silver* (London, 1972), pp. 66–7, fig. 5.

61 *Sunday Independent*, 16th May 1976.

62 T. Fitzgibbon, op. cit., p. 79.

63 E. E. Evans, op. cit., p. 78.

64 K. Danaher, *In Ireland long ago* (Cork, 1969), p. 43.

65 C. Ó'Siocháin, op. cit., p. 78.

66 J. S. Donnelly, *The Land and people of nineteenth century Cork* (London, 1975), p. 245.

67 Quoted in N. Bringeus, 'Man, food and milieu' in *Folk Life*, 8, 1970, p. 45.

6 TRANSPORT

1 Hely Dutton, *Statistical survey of the County of Galway* (Dublin, 1824), p. 148.

2 Sir C. Coote, *Statistical survey of the County of Monaghan* (Dublin, 1801), p. 148.

3 C. E. Browne, 'The ethnography of Inishbofin and Inishshark' in *Proceedings of the Royal Irish Academy*, 3, III, pp. 317–70.

4 Henry Coulter, *The west of Ireland* (Dublin, 1862), p. 83.

5 A. T. Lucas, 'Bog wood: a study in rural economy' in *Béaloideas*, XXIII, 1954, p. 108.

6 Questionnaire on methods of transport, Department of Irish Folklore, University College, Dublin, MS. 1524, *passim*.

7 Ibid.

8 Ibid., p. 66.

9 J. P. Mahaffy, 'On the introduction

of the ass as a beast of burden into Ireland' in *Proceedings of the Royal Irish Academy*, XXXIII, 1916–17, pp. 530–8.

10 W. F. Wakeman, 'Ballydoolough crannóg' in *Journal of the Royal Society of Antiquaries of Ireland*, II, 1870–1, pp. 362–3.

11 A. T. Lucas, 'A hay rope saddle from county Louth' in *Journal of the County Louth Archaeological Society*, XV, 1, 1961, pp. 13–16.

12 E. E. Evans, *Irish heritage* (Dundalk, 1949), pp. 105–13; E. E. Evans, 'Some archaic forms of agricultural transport in Ulster' in W. F. Grimes, *Aspects of archaeology in Britain and beyond* (London, 1951), pp. 108–24; E. E. Evans, *Irish folk ways* (London, 1957), pp. 165–81.

13 A. Fenton, 'Transport with pack-horse and slide car' in Fenton, Podolak and Rosmussen (eds.), *Land transport in Europe* (Copenhagen, 1973), pp. 126–34.

14 E. E. Evans, op. cit., 1951, p. 110.

15 C. E. Browne, 'The ethnography of Clare Island and Inishturk, Co. Mayo' in *Proceedings of the Royal Irish Academy*, 21, 1898–1900, p. 63.

16 A. C. Haddon, *The study of man: an introduction to ethnology* (London, 1898), p. 161.

17 E. E. Evans, op. cit.; G. B. Thompson, 'Some primitive forms of farm transport used in Northern Ireland' in *Ulster Folklife*, 1, 1955, pp. 32–6.

18 G. B. Thompson, op. cit., p. 32; I.F.C., MS. 1524.

19 G. Berg, *Sledges and wheeled vehicles* (Nordiska Museets Handlingar: 4, 1935), *passim*.

20 G. B. Thompson, op. cit., p. 33.

21 R. L. Edgeworth, *An essay on the construction of roads and carriages* (London, 1813), p. 94.

22 A. C. Haddon, op. cit., p. 166.

23 E. E. Evans, op. cit., 1951, p. 119.

24 Ibid., p. 113.

25 A. T. Lucas, 'Prehistoric block wheels from Doogarymore, Co. Roscommon, and Timahoe East, Co. Kildare' in *Journal of the Royal Society of Antiquaries of Ireland*, 102, pt. 1, 1972, pp. 19–48.

26 Ibid., p. 44.

27 F. Henry, *Irish high crosses* (Dublin, 1964), p. 51.

28 D. Greene, 'The chariot as described in Irish literature' in C. Thomas (ed.), *The Iron Age in the Irish Sea Province* (Council for British Archaeology, Report 9,) pp. 59–73.

29 H. F. Berry (ed.), 'Register of wills and inventories of the diocese of Dublin ... 1457–83, 'being an extra volume of the *Journal of the Royal Society of Antiquaries of Ireland, 1896–7*.

30 J. H. Andrews, 'Road planning in Ireland before the railway age' in *Irish Geography*, V, 1, pp. 17–41.

31 P. F. Wallace, 'The organisation of pre-railway transport in Cos. Limerick and Clare' in *North Munster Antiquarian Journal*; P. F. Wallace, 'The development of organised public transport on the roads of Co. Carlow in the pre-railway age' in *Carloviana*, 2, 21, Dec. 1972, pp. 32–6.

32 57 Geo. III, c. 34 (The Poor Employment Act of 1817).

33 *Richard Griffith's report on the roads made at the public expense in the southern districts in Ireland*, H.C. 1831 (119), XII, pp. 4–5.

34 Ibid., pp. 4–5; *Report of Alexander Nimmo, on the western district in Ireland*, 1828, H.C. 1829 (348), XXII, p. 2.

35   I.F.C., MS. 1524, p. 133.

36   J. Hamilton, *Sixty years experience as an Irish landlord* (Dublin, 1894), p. 47, cited in A. C. Haddon, op. cit., p. 196.

37   A. T. Lucas, 'A block-wheel car from Co. Tipperary' in *Journal of the Royal Society of Antiquaries of Ireland*, 82, II, 1952, pp. 140–4.

38   Ibid., p. 135–40; A. T. Lucas, 'Block-wheel car from Slievenamon, Co. Tipperary' in *Journal of the Royal Society of Antiquaries of Ireland*, 83, I, 1953, p. 100.

39   T. Crofton Croker, *Researches in the south of Ireland* (London, 1824), opp. p. 284.

40   H. D. Inglis, *Ireland in 1834* (London, 1834), I, p. 24, cited in A. C. Haddon, op. cit., p. 205.

41   Ivor Herring, 'The "Bians" (II), their place among Irish vehicles' in *Ulster Journal of Archaeology*, 3 S., III, 1940, pp. 115–22.

42   A. C. Haddon, op. cit., pp. 200–18.

43   R. L. Edgeworth, *An essay on the construction of roads and carriages* (London, 1813), pp. 98–101.

44   Ivor Herring, 'The Scottish cart in Ireland and its contemporaries, circa 1800' in *Ulster Journal of Archaeology*, 3 S., VII, 1944, pp. 42–6.

45   E. E. Evans, op. cit., 1957, p. 176.

46   D. Greene, op. cit., p. 63; R. L. Edgeworth, op. cit., p. 100.

47   A. Gailey, 'An English farm wagon from County Fermanagh' in *Ulster Folk Museum Year Book*, 1967–8, pp. 14–16.

7   THE YEAR'S WORK

1   M. Herity, 'Prehistoric fields in Ireland' in *Irish University Review*, Spring 1971, pp. 258–65.

2   R. H. Buchanan, 'Field systems of Ireland' in A. R. H. Baker and R. A. Butler (eds.), *Studies in field systems in the British isles* (Cambridge, 1973), pp. 580–618.

3   E. E. Evans, *Irish folk ways* (London, 1957), pp. 100–14.

4   E. E. Evans, 'Dairying in Ireland through the ages' in *Journal of the Society of Dairy Technology*, 7, 1954, pp. 179–87.

5   A. T. Lucas, 'Cattle in ancient and medieval Irish society' in *O'Connell School Union Record, 1937–58*.

6   J. M. Graham, 'Transhumance in Ireland' in *The Advancement of Science*, X, 37, June 1953, pp. 74–9.

7   Sean Ó'hEochaidh, 'Buailteachais i dTír Chonaill' in *Béaloideas*, XIII (1943), pp. 130–158.

8   R. U. Sayce 'The old summer pastures' in *The Montgomeryshire Collections*, LIV, LV; A. Fenton, *Scottish country life* (Edinburgh, 1976), pp. 124–46.

9   M. Duignan, 'Irish agriculture in early historic times' in *Journal of the Royal Society of Antiquaries of Ireland*, 84, pt. 3, 1944, pp. 130–41; L. Cullen, *Life in Ireland* (London, 1968), pp. 1–19.

10   M. J. O'Kelly, 'Plough pebbles from the Boyne Valley' in C. Ó'Danachair (ed.), *Folk and farm* (Dublin, 1976), pp. 165–76.

11   A. T. Lucas, 'Irish ploughing practices I–IV' in *Tools and Tillage*, II, 1, 1972, pp. 52–62; II, 2, 1973, pp. 67–83; II, 3, 1974, pp. 149–160; II, 4, 1975, pp. 195–210.

12   H. Home, *The gentleman farmer* (Dublin, 1778); G. Rye, *Considerations on agriculture* (Dublin, 1730).

13   J. M. Baker, *Experiments in agriculture* (Dublin, 1769).

14   J. M. Baker, *A short description and list*

*with the prices of the instruments of husbandry made in the factory at Laughlinstown near Celbridge in the county oj Kildare* (Dublin, 1769).

15  M. J. Kelly, *Some old Dublin manu-facturers of farm machinery* (typescript).

16  A. Gailey and A. Fenton (eds.), *The spade in Northern and Atlantic Europe* (Belfast, 1970).

17  P. Campbell, *The hiring* (typescript).

18  J. H. Johnson, 'Harvest migrations from nineteenth century Ireland' in *Institute of British Geographers, trans-actions and papers*, 41, pp. 97–112; also B. Kerr, 'Irish seasonal migration to Great Britain' in *Irish Historical Studies*, III, 12, 1943, pp. 365–80.

19  R. Flower, *The western island* (Oxford, 1946), pp. 102–3.

20  D. Corkery, *The hidden Ireland* (Cork, 1956).

21  T. P. O'Neill, *The state, poverty and distress in Ireland, 1815–45* (unpublished Ph.D. thesis, N.U.I. 1971).

22  A. Gailey and A. Fenton (eds.), op. cit.; C. Ó'Danachair, 'The spade in Ireland' in *Béaloideas*, 1963, pp. 98–114

23  E. E. Evans, *Irish folk ways* (London, 1957), pp. 138–9.

24  A. T. Lucas, 'Furze: a survey and history of its uses in Ireland' in *Béaloideas*, 26, pp. 1–203.

25  J. C. O'Sullivan, 'Slanes: Irish peat spades' in A. Gailey and A. Fenton (eds.), op. cit., pp. 221–42.

26  A. T. Lucas, 'Bog wood: a study in rural economy' in *Béaloideas*, 23, pp. 71–134.

27  A. Fenton, op. cit., illustration p. 138.

28  T. P. O'Neill, 'Some Irish techniques of collecting seaweed' in *Folk Life*, 8, 1970, pp. 13–19.

29  A. T. Lucas, 'The communal collec-tion of sand eels in Ireland' in

*Festschrift für Robert Wildhaber* (Zurich, 1972), pp. 376–87.

30  K. McNally, *The sun-fish hunt* (Belfast, 1976).

31  *Census of Ireland, 1831* (Clare), p. 134.

32  *Times Pictorial*, 10th October 1942; A. McCelland, 'The nailers of Warren-point' in *Ulster Folklife*, 13, 1967, pp. 79–80.

33  J. C. O'Sullivan, 'The tools and trade of the tinker' in C. Ó'Danachair (ed.), *Folk and farm* (Dublin, 1976), pp. 200–8.

34  M. McCaughan, 'Flax scutching in Ulster: techniques and terminology' in *Ulster Folklife*, 14, 1968, pp. 6–13.

35  S. P. O'Ríordáin, 'A pole lathe from Borisokane' in *Journal of the Cork Archaeological and Historical Society*, 48, 1943, pp. 154–5.

36  S. Murphy, *Store mad* (Dublin, 1950).

37  Rev. A. L. Shaw, *Parish of Killoughy* (Killoughy, n.d.), p. 48.

## 8  PLAY

1  E. Brady, *All in! All in!* (Dublin, 1976).

2  A. C. Haddon *The Study of man* (London, 1898), p. 219.

3  Mucklagh N.S., notebook 1.10.37–1.10.38, I.F.C., MS. 805.

4  See example in National Museum of Ireland made by William Monks, Esq., Nevitt, Lusk, Co. Dublin (F. 1948: 228).

5  A. C. Haddon, op. cit., pp. 277–82.

6  E. MacWhite, 'Early Irish board games' in *Éigse: a journal of Irish studies*, V. 1, pp. 25–35.

7  E. MacLysaght, *Irish life in the seven-teenth century* (Cork, 1950), p. 32.

8  J. Huizinga, *Homo ludens: a study of the play element in culture* (London,

1949), pp. 179–80, quoted in T. M. Owen, *Welsh folk customs* (Cardiff, 1959), pp. 21–2.

9   A. Gailey, *Irish folk drama* (Cork, 1969).

10  T. P. O'Neill, 'Irish trade banners' in C. O'Danachair, *Farm and folk* (Dublin, 1976), pp. 177–99.

11  *Sunday Independent*, 1st December 1974; *Irish Times*, 10 December 1974.

12  J. C. O'Sullivan, 'St. Brighid's Crosses' in *Folk Life*, XI, 1973, pp. 60–81.

13  K. Danaher, *The year in Ireland* (Cork, 1972), pp. 13–37.

14  T. G. F. Paterson, 'Harvest customs in County Armagh' in *Ulster Journal of Archaeology*, 7, 1944, pp. 109–16.

15  A. Gailey, 'The last sheaf in the north of Ireland' in *Ulster Folklife*, 18, 1972, pp. 1–33.

16  T. F. Ó'Sullivan, 'Pattern day at Saint Molings' in *Irish Times*, 8–9 July 1976.

17  K. Danaher, op. cit.

18  M. MacNeill, *The festival of Lughnasa* (Oxford, 1962).

19  S. O'Súilleabháin and R. Th. Christiansen, *The types of Irish folktale* (Helsinki, 1963).

20  F. O'Neill, *Music of Ireland* (Chicago, 1903), *O'Neill's Irish music for piano or violin* (Chicago, 1915).

21  A. Gailey, 'Straw costume in Irish folk customs' in *Folk Life*, 6, 1968, pp. 83–93.

22  P. Ó'Tuathail, 'Folk-tales from Carlow and West Wicklow' in *Béaloideas*, VII, 1937, pp. 65–6.

# Index and Glossary